Into Your Hands

Michael Bernard Kelly was born in Melbourne in 1954. He held professional qualifications in theology, spirituality, education and creative media. He was a freelance writer, speaker, activist, counsellor and educator, specialising in spirituality, sexuality and human integration. His ministry included creating rituals, speaking at conferences, leading retreats, offering spiritual direction, and writing for journals, newspapers and books in Australia, the US and the UK. Michael died in November 2020.

Andrew Brown studied religion and sexuality at the University of Michigan, in part to deepen his understanding of his own experiences as a gay Catholic. He received a master of social work from Washington University in St. Louis. In 2015, Andrew moved to Melbourne for a research position in community-led health and wellbeing at Deakin University.

Into Your Hands

Essays Inspired by Mystic, Prophet, and Activist
Michael Bernard Kelly

edited by
Andrew Brown

*

with a foreword by
Ro Allen

Clouds of Magellan Press | Melbourne

ISBN: 978-0-6453531-6-7

Clouds of Magellan Press
www.cloudsofmagellanpress.net

Distribution by John Reed Books, and eBook Alchemy.

Cover image: *The Hand of Job*, Eureka O'Hanlon
http://eurekamichael.blogspot.com/

Acknowledgement of Country

Into Your Hands was compiled and edited on the unceded sovereign lands of the Wurundjeri Woi-wurrung peoples of the Kulin nation. We acknowledge the spiritual connection of First Nations people to Country and pay deep respect to Elders past and present who, for more than two thousand generations, have kept their culture and communities strong through ritual, story and the sharing of sacred wisdom.

Father, I abandon myself into your hands.
Do with me what you will,
Whatever you may do, I thank you.

Charles de Foucauld

Contents

Foreword

Ro Allen

When navigating through the bounds of religion, sexuality and gender identity, it can be hard to grapple with how to reconcile these parts of oneself; shame and fear often go hand in hand with religious beliefs, leaving many of us feeling less than worthy. Because of this, identifying openly as lesbian, gay, bisexual, trans, gender diverse, intersex and/or queer (LGBTIQ+) while also being a person of faith can feel insurmountable. This is a dual identity that I am all too familiar with, and a heartbreaking situation which I have seen drive people to the depths of despair.

Michael Bernard Kelly was courageous in leaning into his identity as a Catholic gay man. In co-founding the Rainbow Sash Movement, Michael openly challenged the Church's treatment of LGBTIQ+ people and was committed to making access to the Church more freely available to people on the margins. It is truly inspiring that he dedicated his life to developing creative approaches to integrate sexuality and spirituality. He refused to sacrifice the parts of himself that the Church didn't approve of, insisting on his right to live as his full, authentic self. He was a true spiritual warrior with abiding faith and boundless resilience. When I served as the Victorian Commissioner for LGBTIQ+ Communities, I observed first-hand how Michael's work had influenced the scholarship around spirituality and sexuality, and in turn how this positively impacted the lives of LGBTIQ+ people of faith.

This collection of essays is a heartfelt tribute to his work and solidifies his legacy as one of Australia's leading gay activists and religious commentators. The authors have carefully interlaced personal memoirs of Michael with poignant reflections on the communion between religion and sexuality. In all, this collection superbly captures the depth of Michael's spirit, defiance and his wholehearted commitment to supporting LGBTIQ+ people to reclaim and transform their spiritual lives. As an LGBTIQ+ person of faith, I am endlessly grateful for Michael's activism. It was an honour to know Michael and I have no doubt he is enjoying himself up there.

Ro Allen
Victorian Equal Opportunity and Human Rights Commissioner
Inaugural Victorian Commissioner for LGBTIQ+ Communities

Introduction

Andrew Brown

This collection of essays brings together a small, but diverse, sample of the community of people connected with and influenced by Michael Bernard Kelly (1954-2020). The range of people who contributed to this collection represents just how wide and deep Michael's impact was and continues to be.

In 2016 a mutual friend recommended Michael Kelly as a significant point of contact within the gay community when my partner, Chris, and I moved from the USA to Melbourne. My first memory of Michael is how he immediately took it upon himself to give Chris and me what he called our 'gay education'. He seemed to revel in this. Whenever we were together, at least once Michael would reference something that he was sure we would be familiar with by virtue of our sexuality, only to express great shock that we were ignorant on the subject, whether it be a particular gay activist, a movie, a scholar, significant writings on queer theology, or key historical events. While Michael's role as 'teacher' quickly developed into something of an inside joke, the knowledge and wisdom he shared will stay with me for the rest of my life.

While Michael did indeed share a great deal of wisdom with me, I would also like to recognise the complex, rich threads that came together to form our relationship that also reflect aspects of Michael's personality and his relationships with others. Michael was one of my first real friends in Melbourne, and was the first person I truly connected with here who had a deep connection with both Australia and the US. Our conversations about the States ran from deep, about politics and spirituality, to fun, as Michael revealed his passion for sweet pies, and in particular pumpkin pies. The last time I saw Michael in person, Chris and I brought him two pumpkin pies that Chris had made from scratch at home. Michael delighted in sweets, and in particular sweets that can be hard to come by in Australia but are plentiful in the US. Michael was key in bridging Australia and the US for me and in establishing Australia as a home.

More than just providing a gay education and helping me settle into Australia, Michael established a deep, two-way relationship in which he was a mentor to me, particularly because he gave me my first true spiritual home in Australia via the Emmaus community. The Emmaus community was established in 2014 by Michael, Irene Wilson and John Xavier Rolley to explicitly celebrate the unique gifts of the LBGTIQ+ community and other groups marginalised by the Roman Catholic Church. These gifts are vital to transform the Church for all, addressing and healing past injustices and ongoing oppressive acts by its hierarchy. Mentoring me and bringing me into the Emmaus community reflected Michael's particular passion and talent for mentoring young people, and particularly young gay men. I feel blessed to have experienced this myself firsthand, giving me insight into just how much he impacted so many people.

Michael's life was not easy, for a wide range of reasons. And yet, rather than succumbing to challenges, Michael consistently found ways to turn them into opportunities. Throughout his life, he challenged an oppressive Church to embrace God's Truth about gender, sexuality, and inclusion more broadly, even as elements within that Church did everything possible to obstruct or silence him. His life was greatly impacted by chronic fatigue syndrome, robbing him of so many opportunities in spiritual leadership but forcing him to confront the holy darkness of the mystical path. Michael's cancer diagnosis was devastating for him and for everyone around him. We lost Michael's physical presence (even as his spirit lives on) much too soon. And yet, even as he learnt to move with the unpredictability of cancer, to 'dance' with it as he would say, and with the complications of the COVID-19 context, he persevered in staying connected to his loved ones and his beloved Mornington Peninsula.

Michael's fidelity to the mystical path, in both its agonies and consolations, was the ground from which he spoke prophetically and courageously in the marketplace, calling his own Catholic and broader church community to account, calling us all to a transfigured understanding of self-giving love. Michael the Mystic delved deeply into all things Christian and all things erotic, seeking deep presence and connection with the world as it was and what it could be in striving for the divine, moving closer to the light. Michael the Prophet took all the fruits of his contemplative heart and shared them with the world. Michael the Activist had a powerful and inspired voice from the margins, which he used to call us back to the radical heart of the tradition. He truly was a thoughtful, wise person and excellent teacher. But he also had a great sense of humour, was very creative, and had a fiery commitment to standing up for what he believed in.

The contributors to this collection engaged with Michael in very different contexts. An example of this diversity of engagement begins with the title and the image on the cover. The title of this collection, *Into Your Hands: Essays Inspired by Mystic, Prophet, and Activist Michael Bernard Kelly* arose from many conversations about Michael and how to best represent this collection of essays. The epigraph, a favourite prayer of Michael's, is based on the final words of Jesus in Luke 23:46. The ideas in the title and epigraph speak to the profound trust, love and surrender that characterised Michael's living and dying. It also reminds us that his legacy is now in the hands of the many people whose lives Michael touched.

Noelene Kelly, Michael's sister, suggested the final book title, while contributor and one of Michael's close friends, Jim Nickoloff, suggested describing Michael as a mystic and prophet in the subtitle. *Activist* was added as well to reflect Michael's commitment to taking action for positive change. Noelene was also deeply engaged in the conversations to decide on the book cover. Noelene played a crucial editorial role in this collection, encouraging and supporting contributors and me to create something beautiful together celebrating Michael. She modelled for me how to hold space for all the contributors to share about Michael's legacy in their own voice, while providing skilled guidance so each voice came through as clearly as possible.

The cover image, entitled *Hand of Job*, is a work of art by Eureka O'Hanlon. The choice of image reinforces the concept of *Into Your Hands*, as Eureka's work, here and in other of his images, displays the beauty and complexity of the male body in its entirety, and it often engages with Catholic themes. The themes of Eureka's work spoke deeply to Michael, but also, Michael was able to offer Eureka inspiration as his art developed. Michael loved the *Hand of Job* and had it hanging in his home. In the context of this book, it represents the way we are all seeking to live in community, always reaching forward and moving through life seeking Truth, Beauty, and Love. The combination of title, cover image, and epigraph resulted from the contributions of several people committed to continuing to live out Michael's legacy. This entire collection of essays represents the collective effort of so many people and is a concrete example of us trying to live out the call 'Into Your Hands'. Michael may be physically gone, but his legacy will live on in our hands as we continue to build the world he worked so hard to create.

No matter how many words I might try to write about Michael, it is impossible of course for me to create a complete picture of him. Indeed, that task would be impossible for any single person because of Michael's many complex facets and his impact on the world. There are broad themes explored by the essays gathered here, but you will also find more specific discussions on the queering of sainthood; on the rereading of mystical texts from a visceral, queer and fully incarnational perspective; on how Michael's honouring of the body intersects with academic discourses such as 'contemplative ecopoetics'; on how theology is transformed when it moves beyond a heteronormative lens and how a focus on the marginalised and dispossessed within our faith communities can transform and liberate the liturgical imagination. You will find here essays that fall into the category of memoir, that reflect in highly personal ways on Michael's lasting impact on individual lives. You will also find essays that engage in an exploration of ideas – both theological and academic – and that extend Michael's insights into new fields of exploration.

Taken together, these essays represent an intriguing insight into a complex, gifted and unique figure. Their diversity in terms of style and perspective underscores the fact that only a range of voices can begin to speak to who Michael was and the nature and efficacy of the legacy he bequeaths to us. Only a range of voices can begin to sing up aspects of the man we all love.

Andrew Brown

Michael Bernard Kelly Biographical Timeline

1954   Born 27 July in Middle Park, an inner-city seaside suburb of Melbourne, Australia. Michael is the fourth child born to parents Bernie and Marge Kelly (both dec.). Michael's older siblings are John (dec.), Maureen and Brian. Michael's younger sibling is his sister, Noelene.

1972   Joins the Order of Friars Minor (Franciscans) in Melbourne. Begins theological studies.

1973   Leaves the Franciscans towards the end of his novitiate year. Remains in Sydney, working odd jobs and lives with the Gates family.

1974   Returns to Melbourne late this year.

1975   Teaches at Killester College, Melbourne. Continues theological studies part-time.

1976   Teaches at Aquinas College, Ringwood, Melbourne.

1980   Bachelor of Theology Degree, Melbourne College of Divinity.

1984   College Minister, St Leo's College, Box Hill. Graduate Diploma of Education, Australian Catholic University.

1988   Contemplative year on the Mornington Peninsula.

1989   M.A. Spirituality, Holy Names University, Oakland, California.

1990   Campus Minister at Holy Names University. Ordained to the priesthood by Marcia Herndon, the Metropolitan (head bishop) of the Ecumenical Catholic Church of America.

1992   Journeys to Nicaragua. Joins Christian Scharen and members of the Peace Lutheran community Danville, California, in fostering a 'sister-church' relationship with San Francisco Libre, a Catholic parish in an impoverished rural area that embodies the principles of Liberation Theology.

1993   Michael comes out publicly as a gay man in an interview with a local newspaper in Berkeley, bringing his professional and ministerial career in the Catholic church to a close. Returns to Melbourne in July.

1995   Diagnosed with Chronic Fatigue Syndrome.

1995   *The Erotic Contemplative* lecture series is published by Joseph Kramer of Erospirit Institute. Begins Fringe Dwellers community in September, offering a place of welcome and inclusion for those marginalised by mainstream churches. Highly creative and inclusive rituals are offered monthly to the general public, initially based at St Stephen's Church in inner city Melbourne, and later moving to Fitzroy.

1996   Begins a gay men's ritual group.

1998   Co-founds the Rainbow Sash Movement with Nicholas Holloway. The first formal action of the Movement takes place on Pentecost Sunday, St Patrick's Cathedral, Melbourne. Approximately 70 supporters participate in the action.

2005   Scholar in residence at Easton Mountain Retreat Center in New York state for 3 months in 2005 and 2006. Conducts many retreats and workshops at Easton in subsequent years.

2007   *Seduced by Grace* is published by Clouds of Magellan Press. M.A. Creative Media (Screenwriting), Royal Melbourne Institute of Technology, Melbourne. Screenplay based on the book *Love is Stronger than Death: The Mystical Union of Two Souls* by Cynthia Bourgeault.

2010   Consecrated to the Episcopate in the Independent and Old Catholic traditions on 5 December at Easton Mountain Retreat Center. Michael served as bishop to the Community of the Incarnation.

2014   Emmaus Community holds its inaugural eucharist, led by Michael, Irene Wilson and John Xavier Rolley. The Emmaus Community celebrates monthly eucharists marking the liturgical seasons; special events, such as the Midsumma (Pride) Festival; and anointing and healing rituals, including an honouring of those killed or wounded in the Orlando massacre.

2015   Ph.D., Monash University, Melbourne. Dissertation title: *Queer flame of love: re-imagining the Christian mystical tradition in light of the experience of contemporary gay men.* The Incardination of John Xavier Rolley is celebrated by the Emmaus Community - a commitment between John and Michael as his bishop to share ministry and support one another spiritually and pastorally. With encouragement from the Good Shepherd Sisters, Emmaus finds a permanent home in the Crypt at the Abbotsford Convent.

2016   Appointed Adjunct Research Associate at the Centre for Religious Studies, Monash University, Melbourne.

2017   Awarded a Coolidge Fellowship by Auburn Seminary and Crosscurrents Journal. Participates in a month of research, collaboration, and discussion with other scholars at Union Theological College, New York.

2018   Travels and studies in Palestine/Israel for 3 months. Participates in the Scholars' Program at Tantur Ecumenical Institute for Theological Research, Jerusalem. Ph.D. thesis is published by Routledge. *Christian Mysticism's Queer Flame: Spirituality in the Lives of Contemporary Gay Men*.

2019   Emergency surgery in December, NYC.

2020   Diagnosed with stage 4 metastatic cancer in February in Melbourne. Dies and enters deeper into Mystery 14 November.

A Gay Pilgrim's Progress

Jay Michaelson

I can't understand why Michael Kelly was so unusual.

I don't mean that his thought wasn't original or distinctive; it was both. I mean, I don't understand why everyone doesn't see things the same way. *Obviously* the sexual can be both a gateway to the spiritual and a worldly embodiment of it. *Obviously*, it's homoerotic for male mystics to experience *unio mystica* with a male deity. And obviously, as Michael wrote in 2007, 'life as a gay person in the contemporary world, with all of its ordinariness, anguish and beauty, can open us at depth to the journey into the mystery of the Divine.'[1]

Yet of course, none of this is or was obvious. On the contrary, much of this wisdom is often regarded as scandalous, and as a result, Michael experienced a kind of vocational loneliness. While he had many friends, and due to his character, many of those friendships were deep and lasting ones, there were only a few colleagues engaged in the distinctive kind of work that he was doing. Michael was too gay and too sex-positive for mainstream Catholicism, while at the same time being too traditionally religious for the mainstream gay community or even most queer theologians. He charted his own course, and it was often a solitary one.

Then again, that sometimes suited him just fine. He begins the collection of his writings, *Seduced by Grace*, with an account of living as a quasi-hermit for a year (emphasis on quasi, since he took breaks from retreat to visit the pub or enjoy 'a sensuous embrace'[2]). And during the sixteen years that I knew him, he was often at his happiest and most centred when he was alone with spirit. Even in community, at the Easton Mountain centre in New York, he often took time for spiritual solitude, like a more worldly desert father – or, perhaps, a desert daddy.

And to be sure, there were and are other LGBTQ Catholic thinkers who remain, as Michael did, resolutely attached to the

---

[1] Kelly MB, *Seduced by Grace: Contemporary Spirituality, Gay Experience, and Christian Faith* (Melbourne: Clouds of Magellan Press, 2007), xiv.
[2] ibid., 3.

Church, its rituals and doctrines, its history and culture. I think of predecessors like John McNeil and John Boswell, or peers like Robert Goss, Brendan Fay, John Stasio, and Mark Jordan, as well as many non-Catholics who felt similar pulls to the traditional (I think here of our frequent co-conspirator, Patrick Cheng). But there were many more people who resembled that interlocutor in *Seduced by Grace* who says of religion, 'Oh, that bullshit. Why do you bother?'[3]

Michael and I became friends because I've bothered with that bullshit too. For a decade, I, too, worked as a religious LGBTQ activist, founding two Jewish LGBTQ organizations, speaking at various rallies and events, and, like Michael, combining mainstream activist work with non-mainstream queer theology and practice. We were kindred spirits, and Michael was a mentor and a friend. From our first meeting, at the Gay Spirit Culture summit in 2003, to our last, at high tea in New York City shortly after his cancer diagnosis in early, pre-pandemic 2020, Michael was a central presence in my life, even when we were separated by ten thousand miles. I wouldn't have written what is still my most successful book, *God vs. Gay? The Religious Case for Equality*, without Michael's input and example. I wouldn't have worked so diligently to integrate my own sexuality and spirituality without Michael's questioning me about my assumptions and habits. In sum, without Michael's influence and friendship, I wouldn't be the person I am, because that person was formed in large part by him.

And yet, because I worked in the non-Orthodox Jewish community, and he in the Catholic Church, our activist narratives diverged. To oversimplify, my team won and his didn't. The conservative Jewish movement, where I did much of my activist work, eventually saw the light and now ordains, includes, and celebrates queer and trans people. America adopted same-sex marriage, thanks both to smart activist lawyering and decades of work on the ground, and the American LGBTQ movement has since evolved, as younger, more trans-and-genderqueer, less white, less cis-male, more intersectionally-oriented voices are now deservedly being centred. (Michael's work was overtly and intentionally grounded in gay male experience, but unlike many of

---

[3] ibid., 89.

his contemporaries, he recognized that and understood that position quite consciously.)

The same transformations did not occur in the Catholic milieu. Despite Pope Francis's various encouraging statements regarding gays and lesbians, the kind of inclusion, respect, and dignity which Michael demanded twenty-five years ago is still not forthcoming. After he was fired and refused communion for speaking his truth and for demanding that queer Catholics be treated with dignity, he was a priest without a parish, and remained so until the end of his life. Michael moved on, pursuing ordination in a non-Roman Catholic church, getting his doctorate (writing on the lives of gay men who, like him, refused to surrender their faith because the institutional guardians of that faith refused them[4]), and finding his way as a not-quite-academic, but academically minded independent theologian.

There was always a tension in Michael's work between its inclusion-focused and more-radically oriented aspects. On the one hand, Rainbow Sash was demanding simple recognition of gay Catholics – Michael and other Rainbow Sash members were publicly refused communion for the sin of expressing their own homosexuality or their support of queer people. In this work, Michael helped hundreds of people directly, and thousands more indirectly – often young and not-so-young people struggling for acceptance or some kind of integration of their spiritual and sexual selves. On the other hand, Michael's work also included more radical, sex-positive, and transgressive elements. I often thought, as Michael was so outspoken and so bitterly condemned for his relatively moderate work, what his persecutors would have thought if they watched *The Erotic Contemplative* (1995),[5] or joined Michael in a Body Electric ritual.[6]

---

[4] Kelly MB, *Christian Mysticism's Queer Flame: Spirituality in the Lives of Contemporary Gay Men* (New York: Routledge, 2018).

[5] The entire video series is now online at https://www.youtube.com/channel/UC6whUXSbW2v22D_WxPZpCPQ and in book form: Kelly MB, *The Erotic Contemplative: Reflections on the Spiritual Journey of the Gay/Lesbian Christian* (Melbourne: Clouds of Magellan, 2021).

[6] The Body Electric School was founded in 1984 in Oakland, CA by Joseph Kramer, PhD. The Body Electric is the largest worldwide, non-governmental community network offering safe sex education and erotic

So, Michael and I became drag queens. We were ero-spirit siblings at Easton Mountain, we were collared-up clergy at rallies, we were somewhat frustrated alt-academics at conferences and panels, we were outsiders passing as insiders when we visited traditional religious environments. These worlds were small and fragmented. To paraphrase the queer theologian Marcella Althaus-Reid, Michael was 'a theologian who learned to survive with several passports.'[7]

Sometimes, these worlds intersected; other times, they did not. For myself, I tended to keep my lives at Easton Mountain, Body Electric, the Radical Faeries, Fire Island, and Burning Man separate from my more mainstream activist work. Michael did not: *Seduced by Grace* intersperses essays about the harm caused by homophobic Catholic bishops with an account of an anal pleasure workshop he attended. Maybe he just had less patience with closets than I.

As I have discussed at length elsewhere in the context of Robert Goss's work,[8] these different worlds – ways of being, even – were also, sometimes in conflict with one another. Arguing for inclusion – allow queer and trans people into the Church, reread the 'clobber texts' of the Bible, celebrate love, and so on – is quite different from rereading John of the Cross as a homoerotic mystic. It's not about the Queer Christ. And it's not about the more radical project of questioning Christianity's and Judaism's core patriarchal commitments. [9] Those efforts, and many more like them, belong to

---

massage. In 1992, Body Electric expanded to become the Erospirit Research Institute, a thinktank exploring the connection between spirituality and sexuality.
https://en.wikipedia.org/wiki/Joseph_Kramer_(sexologist)
[7] Althaus-Reid M, *The Queer God* (New York: Routledge, 2003), 7.
[8] Michaelson J, 'Queer Theology and Social Transformation Twenty Years after Jesus ACTED UP', *Theology & Sexuality*, 21:3, 189-197, DOI: 10.1080/13558358.2015.1222675 (2015).
[9] 'No serious historian could deny that the Catholic Church's history of dealing with homosexual people has been bloody and brutal,' writes Michael in the aptly titled essay 'How a sorry church still destroys so many lives.' Kelly MB, *Seduced by Grace: Contemporary Spirituality, Gay Experience, and Christian Faith* (Melbourne: Clouds of Magellan Press, 2007), 107.

a different tendency of LGBTQ religious work, one that has a more radical, transformative orientation. And yet Michael did both.

The tensions are magnified the closer one looks. Was Michael basically a normative gay man, seeking to reform traditional religion and still go to mass? Or was he a more radical queer person who blames Western religious traditions for centuries of sex-negativity, misogyny, persecution, and death? Both, of course – but not many people are like him. Moreover, good academics make things complicated; the truth lies in imbricated shades of grey, infinite gradations of meaning, subtlety, nuance, and complexity. To queer is to complicate, to problematize, to undermine, to unsettle. Activists, on the other hand, simplify. We need elevator pitches, tag lines, sound bites, and tweets. Love is Love. Born this Way. Activists are interested in the utility of truth to make change in pursuit of justice, not the nuances of complex truths that are difficult if not impossible to communicate.

Mainstream LGBTQ religious activism is there to reassure worried parents that they can love their gay sons and still go to church. In fact, we are there to persuade them that if they go to church, they *ought* to love their gay sons, because that's the Godly thing to do. But radical queer religious activism has more revolutionary ideas. Michael didn't hesitate to associate the Virgin Mary with the Divine Feminine in other traditions, for example. Moreover, he insisted, even the traditional God is already quite queer: butch Jesus, femme Jesus, mystical Jesus, Daddy Jesus. All of these, for Michael, were aspects of the cataphatic way, the mystical path that embraces the world, and eros.

Of course, both Michael and I tailored our theological utterances to the demand of the moment. If I'm in a pastoral role, a chaplain at a hospital, say, and a parent wants me to pray with them for God to heal their child, I am not going to respond by critiquing the notion of intercessory prayer. I'm going to get down and pray with them. Likewise, if I am fighting for gay Christian kids in repressive environments, I will willingly closet my radical theology in order to hopefully lessen their suffering. As I said above, I think I had more patience with this than Michael did, though he did it when he had to, which was often.

Michael's work was also unlike that of most queer theologians in that it was grounded in a mystical, personal faith. This comes through again and again in his writings, just as it did in his life. Remember when that acquaintance asked (at a San Francisco wine bar, in fact) why Michael bothered with 'that bullshit'? His answer, in the 1999 essay 'Gay and Christian: why bother?' is profound in its honesty. First, Michael amplifies the question: 'Are we colluding in our own oppression? What kind of Christianity is not destructive but life-enhancing? Why not just get out and get a life?'[10]

After slamming those who remain by squelching themselves to fit in ('Be nice, be quiet, be discreet,' they say; Michael's response is 'this is not Christian, not healthy, not just, not spiritual, and not the way forward.'[11]), Michael proceeds to give two perfectly good answers. First, there is a response 'that is defiant, that proclaims the right to a place and a voice, that refuses to surrender to the bigots in this complex and rich phenomenon called 'Church." Second, there is the response of activism, fighting to transform an institution 'because they believe the Church has both the call and the potential to be a critical voice for justice and freedom in our society.'[12] It's not just about wanting to go to mass; it's about believing in the power and potential of this gigantic organization of human beings, and fighting to turn it to the good. But then Michael takes a surprising turn:

> Underlying all of this, however, is something deeper, something that has to do with love and faith. In the end, those of us who go through the struggle of integrating their faith with their sexuality do so because they believe in both.... [L]esbian and gay Christians have come to experience deep in their hearts, and in their spiritual loving, something of the love and inner freedom that Jesus spoke of. In living out our faith and being true to our sexuality we believe that we have known, however tentatively, the

---

[10] ibid., 90.
[11] ibid.
[12] ibid., 91.

gracious, guiding presence of Divine Love... This, in itself, is a miracle of grace.[13]

I love this creed so much, it moves me to tears. I love its honesty; its emotional, trans-rational truth; its speaking of faith when most reflective people remain silent. Mysticism, like eroticism, is traditionally kept secret; it has always been this way. And whatever link may exist between the two is a secret within a secret. Yet Michael revealed it all. Ultimately, what keeps us doing this work is love, or Love, or the insistence that the two are the same thing.

Incidentally, even in his mysticism, Michael found a way to be contrarian. Most mystics, if they bother to be mystics at all, turn from the world and toward the Ultimate. In scholarly terms, they take the apophatic approach, or *via negativa*, stripping away everything but God from their consciousness. This is the dominant strain in Catholic mysticism in particular, for example in Meister Eckhart or John of the Cross. Michael, however, was more drawn to the cataphatic, the *via positiva*, which finds and loves God in the world, in all its manifestation and plurality.[14] That was the key, for him: the uniting of the immanent and transcendent, the refusal to leave one for the other. He was a faithful lover and Lover, finding Christ in relationship, eros, justice, variation, and lived human experience. Plenty of people value those things of course, but few do so through a specifically mystical lens, and fewer still through a specifically gay mystical lens, and even fewer through a specifically gay, Catholic, embodied mystical lens. In fact, I think only one person does that, or did.

I want to close, though, on a note of uncharacteristic (for me) optimism. The last two decades of Christianity and Judaism in the West have been sobering for those who value them. The centre is shrinking, rapidly, and the extremes are increasing. At one edge, more young people than ever before in history consider themselves 'Nones' – a category that includes 'spiritual but not religious', atheists, and religious people of no particular denomination or creed.

---

[13] ibid., 92.
[14] Kelly MB, *Christian Mysticism's Queer Flame: Spirituality in the Lives of Contemporary Gay Men* (New York: Routledge, 2018), chapter 2.

At the other, religious extremism is on the rise, whether in the forms of ascendant evangelical and charismatic Protestantism, ultra-Orthodox Jewry, and the more conservative forms of Catholicism that have been ascendant in American political life (and on the Supreme Court) in the last decade. It seems that Christianity and Judaism are shrinking as mass phenomena, with progressive versions of them appealing to fewer and fewer people. But this is actually optimism, I promise. Because while Michael's work exists in a niche within a niche now, in a few decades, niches may be all that is left, certainly for reflective progressive theologies. Especially with each generation seemingly more queer than the previous one, the queer flame of mysticism may well be as appealing a theological orientation as any.

Most importantly, there is the simple fact that Michael was right. He was right to at least muse about whether Jesus was gay, right to unveil the queerness of mysticism. Good queering shows how everything is *already* queer; it's not a process of embellishment, but rather of uncovering – of a kind of epistemological archaeology. This, I think, is what Jay Johnson means when he describes Christianity as a 'peculiar faith' in his book.[15] It is what Marcella Althaus-Reid meant when she described the 'queer God'[16] and what Elizabeth Stuart meant when she said, 'Christianity is a queer thing.'[17] That what we are queering is always-already queer. Perhaps if the persecution of queers by the Church finally erodes, the essential queerness of the Church might resonate anew; there might be thousands of Michaels, Michaelas, and Michaelxs in the coming decades, as the queer erotics of religion are able to better be revealed. Perhaps the Church will indeed 'listen to the wisdom and pain of those who speak about embodiment, erotic grace, radical justice and the incarnate love that flourishes beyond the bounds of the officially

---

[15] Johnson J, *Peculiar Faith: Queer Theology for Christian Witness* (New York: Seabury Books, 2014), 4-7.

[16] Althaus-Reid M, *The Queer God* (New York: Routledge, 2003).

[17] Stuart E, 'Christianity is a Queer Thing', in *Gay & Lesbian Theologies: Repetitions with Critical Difference* (Burlington, VT: Ashgate, 2003), 105-16.

sanctioned 'sacred.'[18] Who knows, maybe on some level that's what the traditionalists know deep down, especially if they wear dresses and red Prada shoes.

I remember just a few years ago, how happy Michael was to be on pilgrimage in the Holy Land, along with all sorts of weirdos and spiritual misfits – in the best parts of that circuit, the misfits outnumber the normals. I remember giving him a bit of advice, having lived in Israel for three years, connecting him to some fellow travellers, and then hearing back how his adventures far exceeded the plans. Here were seekers from diverse spiritual traditions, united not by dogmatic agreement but by the call of spirit, or as Michael once put it, the seduction of grace. It both mattered and didn't matter that Michael was a frocked, defrocked, and refrocked Catholic priest, an erotic contemplative with a gay soul. That was the particularity of his story, and his contribution to the spiritual conversation. But I love to think of him on that pilgrimage, in that liminal zone of seekers, as just another pilgrim with a story, passing through holy spaces in wonder.

---

[18] Kelly MB, *Seduced by Grace: Contemporary Spirituality, Gay Experience, and Christian Faith* (Melbourne: Clouds of Magellan Press, 2007), xiv-xv.

Michael Bernard Kelly: Unbounded Theologian

Beth R. Crisp

Many of the contributions to this volume rightly speak of Michael Bernard Kelly as an activist and advocate. Indeed, it is almost impossible to think of him not being so. However, human beings are multi-dimensional and long before intersectionality became the buzz word, Michael Bernard Kelly was someone for whom the complex interplay of sexuality and spirituality were a daily reality. Moreover, for Michael it was in the everyday when we encounter God rather than just at special events.

Michael's life and work demonstrated that theology is transformed when it moves beyond a heteronormative lens which has sanitised human erotica. In referring to him as an unbounded theologian, I recognise that while he was an Australian whose writing focused on the spirituality of gay men, Michael's work not only traversed national borders, but was part of a growing canon of theological writing which rejected the prioritising of Christian faith and spirituality as necessarily white, heteronormative, cisgendered and disassociated from the body. As such some of the themes in Michael's writings are not dissimilar from those found in the writings of queer, feminist, disabled and non-white theologians.

I first met Michael Bernard Kelly at a conference at St Mary's University College in London in 2009 at which approximately 60 scholars of Christian spirituality gathered. Although not a large conference, there were several eminent theologians present including James Alison, Bernadette Flanagan, David Lonsdale, Bernard McGinn, Gerald O'Collins and Peter Tyler. Fourteen papers, including those by the aforementioned, and Michael Bernard Kelly were subsequently published in *Sources of Transformation: Revitalising Christian Spirituality*.[1] Although perhaps better known by readers of gay theology, the inclusion of Michael's paper in this volume attests not only to the integrity of his writing, but also a

---

[1] Howells E and Tyler P (eds.), *Sources of Transformation: Revitalising Christian Spirituality* (London: Continuum, 2010).

perception by the editors that Michael Bernard Kelly had something to say to a wider audience.

Michael was a writer, with countless publications to his name, including contributions to the gay media, religious media and mainstream press outlets. A selection of such writing, plus letters to family and friends and speeches given by Michael, were published as *Seduced by Grace: Contemporary Spirituality, Gay Experiences and Christian Faith*.[2] Originally published in 2007[3], *Seduced by Grace* provides insights into a man who despite being rejected and marginalised by his church, continued to believe in a loving God:

> In the Church community itself there is still real oppression and it remains true that reputations, careers and lives can readily be destroyed if people are named as gay or even gay-friendly in our Church, despite official claims of tolerance. The imposed silence, the invisibility, the neglect, the exclusion and the active rejection that lesbian and gay people continue to endure in our Church are an insult to the Heart of Christ and a scandal for the People of God.[4]

Like many others over the centuries who have been made to feel unwelcome by the church, Michael Bernard Kelly knew what the prophet Jeremiah meant when he wrote 'Lord you have seduced me, and I have been seduced'.[5] As Michael Kirby wrote in his Introduction to *Seduced by Grace*:

> He cannot let it go because of love. He refuses to let a few powerful old men in frocks divorce him from the Faith that he learned as a boy and that is part of his very essence. He

---

[2] Kelly MB, *Seduced by Grace: Contemporary Spirituality, Gay Experience, and Christian Faith* (Melbourne: Clouds of Magellan Press, 2007).
[3] An updated revised edition of *Seduced by Grace* was published by Clouds of Magellan in 2021. This included one additional piece of writing and some slight textual modifications. References to the text refer to page numbers in the 2021 edition.
[4] Kelly MB, *Seduced by Grace: Contemporary Spirituality, Gay Experience, and Christian Faith* (Melbourne: Clouds of Magellan Press, 2021), 47
[5] Jeremiah 20:7

truly believes that Faith. And he knows that it is a religion of love and equality, with respect for the dignity of each and every one of us.[6]

Being Catholic and being gay were both integral to Michael's identity and not accoutrements that could be chosen to be discarded.[7] Moreover, faith and sexuality were not separate domains but necessarily integrated:

> But first, if we are to be human, to be free, it is essential that we become profoundly open and deeply attentive to our own liminal experiences, and especially in the areas of our sexuality and in our prayer. There can be no true spirituality or growth without this.[8]

Michael considered himself to be a mystic. As I re-read these words, I find myself thinking of another mystic, Julian of Norwich who centuries ago recognised the importance of her bodily existence in her prayer. Hence, it is not surprising when I later find Julian's writings being referred to in *Seduced by Grace*.[9] Another mystic who inspired Michael was Simone Weil who:

> … refused baptism because she felt called to live in solidarity with all those who were outside the officially sanctioned community of the 'faithful'. She insisted that the love of God,

---

[6] Kirby M, 'Introduction' in Kelly MB, *Seduced by Grace: Contemporary Spirituality, Gay Experience, and Christian Faith* (Melbourne: Clouds of Magellan Press, 2021), ix.

[7] See *Seduced by Grace*, 24 where Michael has written 'Can I come fully into the truth of who I am and who I am called to be, can I openheartedly share the gifts and blessings of who I am and how I love, as gay and as Catholic?''

[8] ibid.,7.

[9] ibid., 18 and 203.

the love of Christ, reached far beyond all constructed
boundaries, and she lived and died as a witness to that love.[10]

While directly addressing the need for more contemporary
theological writing which addresses the experiences of gay
Christians, Michael Bernard Kelly's explorations of the integration
of the body and prayer provide encouragement to others for whom
such integration offers a path to hope. I can certainly imagine that
this might include survivors of physical, sexual and emotional abuse,
people with disabilities, and people with eating disorders.

For me, one of the strengths of *Seduced by Grace* is being a
theological work written in Plain English and hence accessible to a
much broader audience than many theological tomes. Yet Michael
could also hold his own in dialogue with other theologians. He
completed a PhD at Monash University, a revised version of which
was subsequently published as *Christian Mysticism's Queer Flame:
Spirituality in the Lives of Contemporary Gay Men*. Moving beyond
his own experiences *Christian Mysticism's Queer Flame* explores the
spiritual journeys of eight North American gay Christians. Aware
that some of the language and concepts would be foreign to some
readers, the Preface includes a subsection 'How to Read this Book':

> I am very aware, however, that for some potential readers, the
> earlier chapters may seem overly theoretical and academic –
> while for scholars in the field much of it may seem quite
> familiar. … Therefore, for readers who wish to engage
> directly and immediately with the spiritual journeys of the
> gay men who invited me into their lives, chapters six and
> seven may be a helpful place to start.[11]

In addition to making a significant contribution to understanding
the lived experiences of self-identified gay male Christians in respect
of their spirituality, *Christian Mysticism's Queer Flame* makes an
important contribution to understandings of the development and

---

[10] Kelly MB, *Christian Mysticism's Queer Flame: Spirituality in the Lives of
Contemporary Gay Men* (New York: Routledge, 2018), 235.
[11] ibid., x.

expression of spirituality over the lifespan. In my own research I have found it easier to find examples of prominent spiritual themes at different life stages than studies of how an individual's spirituality develops and changes as they respond to the challenges of a lifetime:

> At a certain point in their life journeys, each of these men reached a kind of plateau. They had moved through many struggles and awakenings as young gay men of faith; over time they had come out fully and embraced both their sexuality and their spirituality. They now moved into a period of life in which they would be called to live out this integration with maturity and integrity. In service, creativity, study, prayer, and in relationships they would face the hard work of the adult life of faith. Concrete challenges, spiritual gifts, painful lessons, and joyful epiphanies would stretch each man in different ways. He would be confronted with sometimes painful self-knowledge and also by the limitations of others. Through all this, he would learn and grow in unexpected and grace-filled ways.[12]

Michael Bernard Kelly was not just seduced by grace but lived graciously in a world in which many might consider he had motives for revenge, particularly toward the church. He may no longer be with us, but Michael's theological writing is a legacy to all of us who believe that Christian spirituality is not for a privileged minority who believe their lived experience to be representative of humanity.

---

[12] ibid., 207.

Until the Ripples Die

Darren Nash

Teacher. Mentor. Friend. Mick Kelly was all of these. I dare say he was more (he was large, he contained multitudes), but these three are the personae by which I knew him.

I encountered Mick first, as I'm sure so many did, as my teacher at Aquinas College, Ringwood. There was something of a legend around him even then. He was understood to be one of the few 'cool' teachers (we could call him 'Mick', not 'Mr Kelly'!) and – rather more prosaically for us callow youths – he had written the school song. But he was also known to be engaging and unconventional, so I was excited to have him as our English teacher – all the more so when he announced that one of the books we'd be reading that year would be a science fiction novel called *A Canticle for Leibowitz*.

Science fiction was very much my thing, but I never thought to have the opportunity to read it in class. Mick recognised my passion and, rather unexpectedly, my expertise in the field, even going so far as to ask me for a recommendation to take on the Year Eleven Central Australia trip. I was surprised at the time but, of course, I now recognise that this was classic Mick: treating a student like just another adult to be asked an opinion, regardless of their age. (As an aside, it was with special pleasure that in April 2013, thirty-one years after Mick introduced me to *A Canticle for Leibowitz*, I was able to publish a new edition into Gollancz's SF Masterworks series, for which I had become editor at the end of 2010.)

Mick was an extraordinary teacher. I know for a fact that others have compared him with Robin Williams' character in *Dead Poets Society*, so I won't labour that point. I will just say that in the year I was privileged to be in his class I never once heard him raise his voice. He didn't need to. I don't doubt Mick's capacity for anger in a righteous cause but, for us, his disappointment was more potent a tool than any threats of detention or corporal punishment. I have only ever met one other person who was able to inspire in others the same single-minded aim to not disappoint him. Mick was all inspiration, *sans* exasperation, and he brought the subject to life for us, teaching us how to appreciate what we read and improve what we wrote. Put simply, we all did the best we could do to be the best we could be because that's what Mick wanted from – and for – us.

As English teacher, or as director of the Year Eleven musical *Jesus Christ Superstar* – which dominated our penultimate year at Aquinas – he was our mentor, our support, our inspiration and, when the situation demanded it, our champion. We knew Mick was on our side, so long as we were on the right side. I've never known another teacher so willing to face down the system if he felt it was unjust. I am certain that it cost him in terms of career advancement. I am equally certain that he didn't care.

Post-high school, we kept in touch. Parties, small gatherings over a drink or two were enriched by his presence. Although the teacher-student dynamic receded, the imperative to never disappoint Mick remained. Still remains.

Then suddenly, as it now seems, a decade had passed, and I was in England opening a letter from my mother. Accompanying the letter was a newspaper clipping. It was a photo of four gay Catholic men, wearing the rainbow sash, standing before Archbishop Pell, being refused Holy Communion. One of them was identified as 'Michael B. Kelly', and Mum's note wondered if this was the same 'Mick Kelly' who taught me English. At that stage, I didn't know that Mick was gay, and the quality of the photograph wasn't enough for a positive identification, but … well, yes, of course it was Mick. Who else with that name would have the courage to face down one of the highest authorities of the Church in Australia? It was Mick. Of course, it was. Proud of both his faith and his sexuality and unwilling to compromise either. Unwilling to bow to the prejudices of the system, fighting for what was right, no matter the odds. It was Mick.

I had hoped to see him again when we returned to Australia a few years ago, but the prosaic hurdles of modern life made that difficult, with Mick's chronic fatigue adding a layer of complication. Still, there was time. Time for Mick to rest up and for some of his former students – now friends – to arrange their commitments for another occasion. Time to save up the stories and the laughs and the questions. There was time. Until there wasn't.

And here we are, in a world without Mick. Except … Except that's not really true, is it? To quote Sir Terry Pratchett: 'No one is actually dead until the ripples they cause in the world die away'. I remember, as we sat at Mick's funeral, I looked around at the cadre of former Aquinas students and realised that we made up approximately a fifth of the congregation. Every one of us forged in the crucible of Mick's passion and compassion. Every one of us bearing his mark as clearly as a Da Vinci brush stroke on 'The Last Supper'.

And I dare to hope that all of us with children have taken the time to pass on his influence, to tell them of a man we once knew. A man of grace and faith, of deep love and fearsome intellect. A man who challenged us and touched us and inspired us to be the very best versions of ourselves we could be. A teacher, a mentor and a friend.

A man called Mick Kelly.

Towards a Queer Contemplative Ecopoetics

Kate Rigby

One of the great pleasures of supervising doctoral candidates is the journey of discovery that you take with them: one on which, sooner or later, they come to know so much more about their topic than you ever did; one on which, if you are lucky, an enduring friendship might be formed. My journey with Michael Kelly was one such; except that, right from the start, I felt that I was the one being educated. Michael taught me more than I can say, more even, I suspect, than I can know. And even now, when he is no longer with us in the flesh – the flesh, whose frailty he knew all too well, but that he never ceased to honour as integrally a part of God's good creation – the seeds sown in that supervisory relationship continue to sprout in my own work, as well as bearing much fruit in others' reception of his.

Michael was somebody I had wanted to meet long before he asked me if I would mentor his PhD in Religious Studies at Monash University (tipped off, perhaps, by his sister Noelene, whose doctorate in creative writing I also had the immense pleasure of supervising). He first came to my attention through a short essay that I read in Melbourne's *Age* newspaper on the eve of Easter Week in 2000. Entitled 'Jesus gloried in a woman's touch', this exquisite meditation on the story of the woman who, in the weighty days that culminated in the Cross, anointed Jesus's feet with costly scented oils and dried them with her long hair (Matt.2:6-18; Mk 14:3-9; Lk 7:36-50; Jn.12:1-8).

Having been raised in the Church of England, with an interest in the Bible, I was vaguely familiar with this story. But the significance that Michael disclosed in it was an utter revelation to me: one that contributed to my slow, faltering, rapprochement with a faith that I had firmly rejected on account of what I saw (with Nietzsche) as it's betrayal of the earthly in favour of an otherworldly beyond; but one that, as Michael helped me to appreciate, still held transformative spiritual gifts, and emancipatory potentials, long hidden by most churches.[1]

For in Michael's retelling, this strange story, which has never been accorded the place it deserves in the celebration of Holy Week, clearly reveals Christ's affirmation of the 'delight of the senses and the erotic joy of the body', summoning us 'to open our hearts and our bodies to the seduction of grace', and to 'learn, at last, to revere the human body, in all the beauty and sensuality of our living and our loving, in the harsh reality of our suffering and dying, in the wonder of our rising to new life. For here, surely, we find the mystery of Easter.'[2]

The deeply incarnational Christianity, of which Michael gives a glimpse in this little gem of an essay,[3] was one, it seemed to me, that opened a pathway towards the kind of ecospirituality for which I had been longing. But what I came to recognise more fully only after I began supervising his doctoral project, was that it also was pivotal for overcoming the repressive heteronormativity against which Michael had been battling in the Catholic church for several years before this article was published. This was the second way in which Michael had already arrested my attention and aroused my admiration: namely, as one of the courageous co-founders of Melbourne's Rainbow Sash Movement in 1998. One of those whose lives was touched by this movement was a young Catholic priest, who had been participating in the Ecophilosophy in the Pub discussions led by Freya Mathews that I too had joined in the late 1990s, and in whom I had witnessed something of the appalling anguish visited upon gay men in his calling.

---

[1] I am also indebted to some of my other wonderful PhD students for disclosing further facets, especially Anne Elvey, Mark Manolopoulos and Jan Morgan.

[2] Many thanks to Noelene Kelly for sending me the text of this article.

[3] The essay emerged from his influential lecture-series from 1994 on 'The Erotic Contemplative', published posthumously in 2021 (Kelly MB, *The Erotic Contemplative: Reflections on the Spiritual Journey of the Gay/Lesbian Christian* (Melbourne: Clouds of Magellan, 2021)). See also Kelly MB, *Seduced by Grace: Contemporary Spirituality, Gay Experience, and Christian Faith* (Melbourne: Clouds of Magellan Press, 2007).

As Michael's supervisor, I was privileged to gain a deeper understanding of the unjust suffering caused by the church's homophobia, with its toxic mix of official sanction and secretive sexual abuse; but through Michael's own story, and those of the men who graciously agreed to participate in his research, I also learnt of resilience, recovery, and of wellsprings of love, hope, faith and joy that abide or, at least, resurface; and I came to recognise how much the churches have to gain by embracing the earth-affirming, body-embracing, sexually-inclusive spirituality that Michael uncovers here.[4] This is something to which, in a small way, I hope to contribute through my involvement with the Church of England's current process of discernment around identity, sexuality, relationships and marriage, 'Living in Love and Faith'[5]. It is one of the ways in which the journey I embarked upon with Michael all those years ago continues to unfold.

Another way, of course, is in my academic life: in particular, in my exploration of what I have come to term 'contemplative ecopoetics.' In this, I am indebted to the induction into the wonders of the Christian contemplative tradition that I received as Michael's supervisor. Contemplative ecopoetics, in my understanding, embodies a mode of resistance to the instrumental logic of modernity: a form of writing and acting that directs your gaze to things beyond the page that elude your grasp, the inner radiance of which shows up only when approached, as William Wordsworth puts it in 'The Tables Turned', with a 'heart/That watches and receives'.[6]

I think that Michael would have delighted in Virginia Burrus's ecopoetic reconsideration of the Christian contemplative tradition, upon which Wordsworth was in certain respects both drawing and diverging. As she shows, the Desert Fathers and Mothers who

---

[4] Michael's PhD has since been transformed into his marvellous monograph, *Christian Mysticism's Queer Flame of Love: Spirituality in the Lives of Contemporary Gay Men* (New York: Routledge, 2018).
[5] Church of England, 'Living in Love and Faith,' https://www.churchofengland.org/resources/living-love-and-faith (accessed May 4, 2021).
[6] See in particular the first chapter of *Reclaiming Romanticism: Towards an Ecopoetics of Decolonization* (London: Bloomsbury, 2020).

inaugurated it had some seriously queer proclivities (not least, Simeon the Stylite, famed for insisting that his followers collect and return to his open wounds the maggots that had fallen on the ground, so that his flesh would continue to be food for others).[7] None, as far as we know, were openly gay or lesbian, however. Nor have I – as yet – explicitly made the connection between the two strands of Michael's legacy in my own life and work.

In writing this tribute, then, I wish to begin to take up the challenge of doing so by concluding with the words of one of my favourite contemporary contemplative ecopoets, the lesbian author, Mary Oliver, whose own partner, like Michael, succumbed to cancer. Oliver's verse radiates a sensuous delight in the natural world that is inextricably entwined with an empathetic attentiveness to the hazards of creaturely existence, and a (frequently self-ironic) readiness to reach out a hand to other-than-human neighbours in distress. There is no dualism of *eros* and *agape* here, such as has long warped and wounded Christian teaching on love. Yet openly erotic, let alone explicitly sexual, moments are relatively rare. In the collection that bears a photo of the author beside her beloved Molly Malone Cook, to whom Oliver had dedicated book after book, there is nonetheless a luscious little poem in which, in my reading, a non-heteronormative eroticism is gently wedded to a profoundly incarnational ecospirituality. It is called 'Poem: Summer Night', and this is how it ends:

> If I step outside
> I smell the grass, or the rain.
> Or that purse of honey, another one awake –
> the blue iris, so straight, so sweet-lipped.
> Soft and alone in the dark.[8]

---

[7] Burrus V, *Ancient Christian Ecopoetics: Cosmologies, Saints, Things* (Philadelphia: University of Pennsylvania Press, 2019), 123-35.
[8] Oliver M, *Long Life: Essays and Other Writings* (Cambridge MA: Da Capo Press, 2004), 92.

Now that's a poem that I would have dearly loved to ponder with Michael; one that even now, I am reading anew as I contemplate his unfolding legacy in my own life and work.

Until We Meet Again! Memories of Michael

The Gates Family

In 1972, two parents and eight children, being the Gates family, met Michael when both he and I joined a Catholic Order of priests and brothers based on the example and teachings of St Francis of Assisi. Over the next 13 years or so Michael had frequent interactions with my family, staying with us, being at birthdays, weddings and funerals as well as living at our home in the year after he left the Franciscans. Unfortunately, by the 90s, our paths had diverged to the point where we lost touch until 2018 when he contacted my brother Peter about the upcoming Plenary Council and our conversations were reborn.

All my brothers and sisters remember him fondly and feel the loss of his death. Our parents also valued him highly. My brothers Mark and Peter have provided some of their own stories of knowing Michael and they are presented below, following my own thoughts on one of the most influential people in my life. Paul Gates.

Paul

I met Michael early in 1972, at Kew in Melbourne. Along with five others we had joined the Franciscans, inspired to live out the Gospel in a simple and straightforward manner as St Francis of Assisi had done. For 50 years Michael and St Francis have had an influence on me.

That first year with the Franciscans was a seminal period in my life and I dare say Michael's too. We were both freshly out of school, meeting new and remarkable people, transposed to an unfamiliar setting and beginning what we believed would be our life's work of giving ourselves fully to making the world a more peaceful and loving place. Neither of us ended up formally as Franciscans, but Michael certainly helped to bring greater understanding and peace to many, as he had initially set out to do, though not necessarily in the form he imagined back in 1972. But first, before the peace, the internal wars!

Michael seemed to be very friendly after we started to get to know each other in those early months of 72. Perhaps a bit too friendly. As a sheltered, naïve young man from a traditional Catholic family (so was Michael), I was a little put out by Michael's apparent growing fondness of me. Michael, for his part, was a little perturbed that I seemed to be distancing myself from him at times. And so began a time of inner turmoil for both of us, him struggling to come to terms with his feelings for a man and his own sexuality; me struggling to come to terms with my feelings towards his feelings and my own sexuality.

We learnt much from each other about the human condition, both during that turbulent year, and in subsequent years. In fact, only months before he died, he recommended I read *A Question of Truth: Christianity and Homosexuality* by Gareth Moore OP. Michael's own exploration of this area of sexuality and spirituality was part of his life's work and through it he achieved the spread of a great deal of love and justice in our world. St Francis himself would, I'm sure, be proud of Michael's contribution to the welfare and education of all. Many live much happier lives now than they might have done, had such things as the Rainbow Sash Movement and Michael's other work not existed. I am proud of his work.

1973 saw us move to Campbelltown, NSW for our Novitiate year, a time of concentrated exploration of the spiritual life. By the end of 73, Michael left the Franciscans. The next period was quite stressful for him as he sought to reorient what he now wished to do, while still developing his understanding of what it meant to be a young, committed man. Michael stayed for some of this time at my family's home, which is where my parents and siblings got to know him. Here he became famous to us as musician, singer–songwriter, joke teller and philosopher.

In 1974 I returned to Melbourne with the Franciscans. Michael continued my education (this time culturally) as we went to see stage shows, live performances and cult movies – all new to me – and many up-and-coming singers in the coffee shops of the time.

A couple of years later my Dad died and Michael played guitar at his funeral. When Michael's own Dad died I saw a ritual I had not even thought of before, where Michael arranged for shovels to be at the grave and the families and friends were asked to take an active part in filling in the grave if they wished. I found this brought the burial to completion much better than simply walking away from an open grave that someone else would fill in. We used the same idea in the burials of both my wife's Mum and my own Mum. It seemed such a natural thing to do and was an example of Michael's natural gift with ritual and also with understanding peoples' feelings.

Michael was at my wedding to my wife, Tricia, in 1983 and gave us a small Mimovitch bronze statue as a gift. As an artist, Mimovitch sought to capture the bond between the spiritual and the physical worlds, so a very apt gift from Michael. I treasure it still and it sits in our dining room today.

Unfortunately, from the latter 80s we did not see much of each other. Life took Tricia and I to Cairns and the busyness of a young family. Michael spent a number of years overseas, and then, from the mid-90s onwards, returned to the USA almost annually as his work in activism, public speaking, writing and retreat facilitation expanded and evolved.

It wasn't until 2018 that we reconnected properly and took various opportunities to talk, to remember and to speak deeply of our current situations. My great regret is that we were not in more regular contact during these years, sharing each other's company and wisdom.

It was in May 2020, that Michael contacted me and said he had some difficult news to tell me.

In the conversations that followed Michael's cancer diagnosis, we were able to express gratitude for all our years of friendship. As I wrote to Michael in one of my emails, 'You always impressed me with your search for truth and your ability to try to convince others of it. You frequently challenged my own cosy convictions and stretched my mind – and still do! Your sense of humour, sharp insights and musical abilities have put others at ease and enlightened them in a gentle way. (I sang 'Flower of Scotland' to all our children and now I am singing it to the grandchildren. I believe I first heard the song from you).

In the passing of all these years we remained friends. I spoke with him two days before he died. He expressed his feelings that he was fearful but also calm about the prospect of death as being the last part of his life. A life well lived it seems to me and one which has helped make me the person I am today.

I still see his intense eyes, interested, sharp, attentive, as he follows an argument, weighing the sides and then I hear the insightful comments (mind you, I still reckon he was sometimes wrong!). I thank him for his generosity and brave spirit.

To paraphrase an old blessing: 'Michael, until we meet again, may God hold you in the hollow of His hand.'

Peter

I had gotten to know Michael a little in the years my brother Paul and he were in the Franciscans. We were fortunate to make the trek as a family from Sydney to Melbourne to see Paul in the first years at Box Hill. Michael's family kindly let us all stay in their home whilst there. It was lovely that my family could do something similar for Michael just after he left the Franciscans and was living in Sydney. For much of this time he stayed in the Gates family home. This is where I got to know Michael a little more.

One fond memory of Michael during this time was born from the silly notion I had of being Michael's manager for his budding career as a singer-songwriter. I sensed great potential and was keen to see him climb to great 'Neil Diamond' heights. The next Jonathon Livingstone Seagull was not far off!

To this day I am not sure how serious Michael was about it all. He did seem to be totally committed, witnessed by his quite prolific output of new song product, and he was very willing and able to perform his songs for this novice manager. Michael also seemed quite open to and supportive of the idea of this partnership.

Now upon reflection he was most likely simply being kind and generous to my own creative spirit by allowing me to proffer the idea for some months. As most of you would know Michael did write many beautiful and wonderful songs, but was, at least at that time, let down by his 'L' plated manager.

In more recent years I was fortunate to meet up with Michael over email and a few telephone calls. This was initiated in the first instance by an enquiry from Michael about the Plenary Council to be held by the Catholic Church in Australia. Michael had noted that

I was involved in some of the preparations and so made some enquiries. This was 2 or 3 years ago, and Michael was asking what voice the LGBTIQA+ community might have in terms of input to the Council. Importantly it was at a time when the community consultation phase of this process was taking place.

In Melbourne there were a number of *Listening and Dialogue* gatherings where interested people could share with one another and with organisers, the issues and concerns they wanted addressed by the Council. Such sessions were a wonderful example and experience of what Pope Francis has called the Catholic Church to be – a Synodal Church – a Church which listens to all, where people can speak boldly and respectfully, where listening is more than simply hearing. It is a mutual listening in which everyone has something to learn – all listening to each other, and all listening to the Holy Spirit.

Now my recount may be a little inaccurate in the detail, but you'll get the point of this story shortly, I hope. I had mentioned these gatherings to Michael and suggested he might like to be a part of them. I was not sure if Michael was going to attend the upcoming gathering, or indeed, any.

This particular event went ahead and afterwards in speaking with one of the organisers I heard that there were indeed some concerns and challenges for them in holding this particular gathering. It had begun with a fair degree of nervousness for many. Throughout the day though, the proceedings were going along really well and the process of listening and dialogue was being engaged in with wonderful good will. There was a lovely sense of go(o)d spirit.

In the later part of the process there was meant to be an opportunity for sharing back to the whole group the ideas, concerns, suggestions that had been raised in breakout groups. This feedback would help inform the development of an agenda for the Plenary Council itself. At this point, however, there was an initial breakdown in the process. Some of the organisers had left before the important feedback element was completed. You can well imagine some of the rising emotions and concerns of the people gathered. Remaining organisers quickly decided that the process would continue to its appropriate conclusion. And it did!

Right at the very end when one of the facilitators was bringing the gathering to a close, a man stood up and came to the front. In quite a surprising movement, he asked if he could speak. There and then! The facilitator, hopefully remembering the notion of synodality mentioned above, and even though caught off guard and not sure what to do, handed the microphone over to the fellow.

There was one of those short yet seemingly endless and deep silences. Then gently, calmly, prayerfully and with such good spirit, the fellow spoke. He touched the gift and graciousness of those gathered as he shared and prayed. It was a mysterious moment of grace.

The gathering then came to an end but the people stayed and continued to enjoy each other's company and words. They stayed so long, filled with the gift of the moment, that the organisers in the end had to begin to turn off some of the lights to encourage people to move outside the venue.

The man who gently, calmly, prayerfully and with such good spirit 'spoke', was Michael.

Mark

For the record, the Michael Kelly I knew was never going to go quietly into the night!

A man for all seasons; I recall his first part-time job at the newly established McDonalds at Punchbowl as one of the first Ronald McDonalds to charm the public. He didn't like the food but loved the kids and the work.

I cannot think of the word 'gentle' without remembering Michael. His calm, strong, deeply spiritual presence disguised a joyous, rebellious, irreverent, humorous nature that strained against the status quo.

Gifted with a sharp analytical intellect, he craved a better world, a kinder reality in which openness, integrity and vibrant authenticity, being aware of 'Self' and 'Purpose' were reasons to live by.

One of my fondest memories was the long walk along Brighton Beach in Sydney, not Melbourne, after a very enjoyable longer lunch shortly after Michael had left the Franciscans and commenced living with our family at Beverly Hills.

For a kilometre or two he mused on and on about his realisation that he was gay, and the liberation of spirit that had come with that awakening.

As the fourth son in a family of eight very Catholic children raised by quintessential, classically orthodox parents in the arguably homophobic society of the fifties and sixties in Australia, the power and force of his 'Eureka Moment' was not lost on me. However, when he then espoused the 'mysterious' and unknown joy of same sex relations, I recoiled in angst, appreciating the difference between us.

But over time, what Michael truly did for me, and I am certain for many of my siblings, was help us grow morally and spiritually to appreciate that gay or straight, we are all just equal, loved by God and blessed to enjoy the Gift of Faith we shared.

His later heroics in the 'Rainbow Sash' and Cardinal George Pell confrontations, confirmed for me the strength, tenacity and courage of this truly unique and special person. He shared, he communicated, he educated and he loved. Stubborn, strong-willed and determined, a positive agent of change, he was a force to be reckoned with, and his presence will be sadly missed until we meet again.

Vale Michael and thank you for sharing a life so well and fully lived!

Prayer, Pizza, and 'Wonderful Troublemakers'

Abanob Saad

It's hard to write about a person whose legacy and character is greater than words can hold or begin to capture faithfully.

But I guess I'll give it a go.

I met Michael some short years ago at a Listening and Dialogue Session which the Catholic Church ran to seek input from the broader community, queers especially, on key issues to be discussed at their upcoming Plenary Council. Their question, 'What is God asking of us in Australia at the present time?' was rhetorically answered by the men in black in the room as they refused to allow a free-flowing discussion or any semblance of debate on the thorny issue of the role of the Catholic Church now and in the future. Michael and a few brave souls, the 'wonderful troublemakers' as Michael would later call us, stood up to quiz the nonsensical parody we all found ourselves in. Let's just say, the rest of the night was a series of begrudging surface answers to deep questions.

If my memory serves me right, it was Michael who took on the concluding prayer role, of his own accord, praying for healing of the damage wrought on queers by the church; for repentance from the church as it acknowledged its sins, and hope for those in the room.

It was a moving prayer. The only sensible godly thing of the night, dare I say.

This man, humble in demeanour, bubbling around the room with a radiant smile, was one I wanted to meet. Very much so.

Michael was gracious and grateful in the exchange we had. Definitely godly. You can smell that a mile away, and trust me, there are very, very few of the godly ones around.

When I told him I was Coptic Orthodox, he smiled and said it must be very difficult for me to be gay and Coptic, bravely showing myself at this event. I laughed. I argued that in spite of their hot mess, at least the Catholics were openly talking about and acknowledging that queer people are real and alive, that they exist, unlike my people whose heads are so deep in the sand of denial that the pyramids would be more likely to rise and walk before the existence of queer Copts was acknowledged. We shared a sigh.

He encouraged me to press on and not be afraid to be who God created me to be. That was very kind yet painful to hear. For that night, miserably and publicly, brought me to tears as the discussion went on. It touched on the very raw trauma of conversion therapy, and it was mightily hard to hold on. Hearing Michael say such kind words, tending unknowingly to my wounded soul, was an act of grace and compassion. I have never received such words from my church, my people or my community. But here, a firebrand, a godly man, spoke truth.

Michael then introduced me to Dr Maria[1], saying that she's a wonderful person, kind, and a really good friend and ally. I felt like everyone that night knew someone there, while I was like a rookie knowing no one. So, the warm introduction by Michael to Dr Maria is an enduring legacy I cherish and am eternally grateful for. I've most joyfully adopted Dr Maria, democratically so, as my Nonna (she loves it!) and for that gift that Michael kindly shared with me of Maria, I'm forever in gratitude.

The Psalmist says, 'How good and wonderful it is for brethren to dwell together in unity!' and on that humid and hot weeknight, being with Michael and Maria, was an embodiment of that reality.

Not long after, Michael and I shared a pizza over lunch together. Well, it was funny as they got the order wrong and so we didn't have to pay, and they fixed it with a free dessert! Like I told you, this man is a saint, or a 'wonderful troublemaker'.

In our discussion, I expressed my great battle trying to wrestle the forces of faith and sexuality so as not to be killed or consumed by them whole, and I tearfully let him in to the horrific experience of conversion therapy that I was still trying to survive. God, even writing this pains me.

Michael teared up hearing my story and compassionately empathised with the live pain rather than wishing or praying it away. He affirmed that I was normal, good, natural and an intended creation by God, not a woeful mistake, though there are days I find

---

[1] Dr Maria Pallotta-Chiarolli (AM), Honorary Fellow, School of Arts/Education, Deakin University.

it nigh impossible to believe that. He also strongly denounced the evils done in the name of God, which was the first time someone had called out conversion therapy for what it is – evil. I thanked him for the generous support, and we tucked into the right pizza order. It was good.

As a parting gift, he gave me his book, *Seduced by Grace*, and suggested I read the chapter on Emmaus. He noted the two disciples recognised Jesus outside Jerusalem amongst their suffering and pain. In the same way, I will know and recognise Jesus outside my Jerusalem, outside my Copt community, an outsider gay Copt, in and amongst my pain and suffering. This also meant that this period of alienation was not an accident but has purpose. God will be on the lookout for me, Michael added. That chapter, indeed, was helpful to me on my journey.

We kept in contact, on and off, thereafter but I was sure that he prayed for me, supported, and affirmed me. Though Michael is now not with us in the flesh, his memory will be eternal, in his works, life and example.

And for me, Michael's most enduring gift remains in the joyous friendship and kind mentoring of my Nonna, whom he also called a 'troublemaker.'

So, Michael, thank you for this wonderful gift you've left me! We will keep making more 'wonderful trouble' for you!

Mortal Flesh

Mark D. Jordan

During our correspondence, until the very end, I was usually the one who owed a reply. As a writer of epistles, Michael Kelly was tireless—also witty, earnest, agile. His messages moved from incidents of travel or plans for a meal through academic research and publishing into theological questions urgent for both of us. I often envied Michael the obvious energy of his apostolic life as a traveling teacher, leader of retreats, and liturgical presider. (More than once he referred to 'the joys of my itinerant lifestyle.')[1] Despite his schedule, and seemingly wherever he found himself, Michael wrote regularly. I was most regular in my apologies for sluggish replies.

The correspondence was our ongoing connection. It was also a reminder that we had encountered one another mostly through circulated words. After scouring my memory and consulting old journals, I still cannot remember when or where I first shook Michael's hand. I do recall, without prompting, that I first heard his voice, in the late-1990s, through the *Erotic Contemplative* lectures. Launching a correspondence, we returned to that original contact through messages sent out—though never at the same pace.

We differed in more significant ways, which our correspondence sometimes tried to name. The point was not to quarrel. When we reflected on versions of our selves, we aimed to appreciate each other more candidly.

We diverged over churches. Before we began exchanging emails, I had fled Roman Catholic institutions. I took with me gratitude for an intellectual formation by Latin-speaking Christianity. (Thomas Merton and Thomas Aquinas both sparked my desire to write theology, and the Eucharist anchored abstract prayers.) But I had concluded that the contemporary Roman 'magisterium' stood ready

---

[1] For example, email from Kelly to Jordan (and Julie Byrne), January 12, 2016. In what follows, I cite our correspondence parenthetically by date. Permission to share correspondence has been granted by Noelene Kelly on behalf of the estate of Michael Kelly.

to jettison any obstacles to its cultivation of power, whether basic virtues or deep traditions. Michael saw just as sharply the failings of Roman Catholic structures. He had travelled his own distance from them. Still, he continued to believe what he had emphasized at the conclusion of *Erotic Contemplative*: like the disciples who finally recognize Jesus in Emmaus, we are obliged to return to 'our' churches to declare that we have seen the Lord risen in flesh.

Michael's balance of exodus and return, of an expulsion answered by a gift of good news, was not easy to describe. He was generous but hardly credulous. After he decided to accept ordination in an independent Catholic lineage, he had a dream: 'it was made clear to me that in no way was I ever again to be a 'supplicant' before the structures of the church' (12/20/15). But the dream's assurance came with a question: 'Could it be that there are people who need me to stop petitioning Rome … and be the priest I am called to be, that I have always been called to be?' A month earlier he had written: 'I probably share many of the misgivings you would have about various kinds of obsession with apostolic succession, and certain understandings of the meaning and importance of ordination itself—and yet, and yet … there continues to be power in prayer and the laying on of hands' (11/17/15). We agreed on the healing power. It was the 'and yet' that pulled us some ways apart. For me, the 'and yet' that raises up priests and prophets within churches also rebukes churchly efforts to manage them. The laying on of hands cannot be confined by jurisdiction.

Michael and I also parted when it came to drawing practical lessons from theological insights. Re-reading our emails, I am struck by how often we could agree on an articulation only to disagree in its enactment. Once Michael wrote of his 'gentle obsession with trying to bring Christian mysticism and gay experience into creative engagement' (4/16/15).[2] This led him to experiment with forms of contemplative community. Impelled by the same obsession, I stayed in seminar rooms and libraries to find or make better words. I didn't

---

[2] In our correspondence, as in *Erotic Contemplative*, Michael spoke most often about 'gay men'. Sharp questions can be raised about both terms in that phrase or about their combination. But let me respect Michael's habits of speech.

want tidier classifications or stricter principles. I rejected most existing languages for sex and gender because they reduced embodied situations to cases under a rule. Crucial encounters in our lives are never instances. Earnest prayer—even using memorized words—is measured by a body's unrepeatable heartbeats.

The friendly divide in our 'careers,' our church affiliations, and our obsessions points to a distinction in our relation to the root of language. We were both lured by theological words close to skin, but the words we followed were not the same. Nor were our ways of saying and unsaying them. Instructed by Western mystical traditions, Michael knew the importance of apophasis or 'negative' theology. He describes it vividly in *Erotic Contemplative* under the paired images of desert and darkness. Still, he remained optimistic about people's abilities to report their sexual and spiritual experiences. By the time we began to correspond, we had each spent years conducting interviews with gay-identified men about their lives. Michael used the transcripts 'to explore in depth the real spiritual lives that are being lived by such men, including the ways they have worked to integrate sexual desire, play, expression, darkness, intimacy … I am saying that openly gay, sexually expressive gay men are already living deep Christian spiritual/mystical lives' (8/11/10). Those interviews anchored his dissertation and then a book. Compiling my own interview transcripts, I kept noticing how far our readiest words stray from our 'real spiritual lives,' how quickly we fall back on the scripts settled by churches, 'liberation' movements, pop songs, advertising. How hard it is to find fresh words for the oldest longings.

I'm not faulting Michael's skill as an interviewer. He was better at it than I was. He had an eye for the tricks of power lurking in friendly questions. He could encourage without leading and reassure without presuming to judge. Still, or therefore, he was less suspicious of language. He worried less than I do about the rhetorical ghosts that haunt familiar labels and approved slogans.

I am tugged towards Michael's projects. I want to enlist. Couldn't I borrow a little of his confidence to declare that we were animated after all by one and the same theological hope? Certainly, we both hoped that some Christians would recognize human intimacy—its bodily pleasures, its vulnerability and generosity—as occasions for revelation. ('Sex as teacher,' he repeated.) We imagined that centuries of Christian polemic against sex could now yield to fully incarnational theology, that erotic language for divine encounter need not remain allegorical, that sin (wherever it really lurked) could never obliterate the goodness of created pleasures. Still, the little archive of our messages displays contrary dispositions to language, especially around sex. As if the body's imminent surrender to breaths, moans, cries called for special care in the choice of words just before.

If we didn't join together under one project, we did share a practice: we wrote. Michael said, 'My work will always be experimental and somewhat creative' (10/19/15). Writing forbidden theology requires *poesis*, that is, making new categories and cautions but also new characters for emerging ways of life and new ethics to promote their flourishing. Even at their most relaxed, many people cannot speak their sexual lives without giggling, blushing, seducing, or boasting. Imagine, then, the ferocious inhibitions on candid speech about sexual episodes as divine instruction.

In a little book with a lot of sex in it, Sarah Manguso remarks: 'Nothing is more boring to me than the re-re-restatement that language isn't sufficiently nuanced to describe the world. Of course language isn't enough. Accepting that is the starting point of using it to capacity. Of increasing its capacity.'[3] Michael and I agreed about that too, not just as aspiration but in practice. I mean, we kept on writing.

Languages are made by and for communities. New religious and erotic groups coalesce around new names.

Over decades, Michael led communities of various sizes. He was hopeful about shaping a new one during the years of our correspondence. It would be a gathering of gay men intent on recognizing the connection between the pursuit of a fleshed God and other (queer) loves. Michael kept 'nurturing this embryonic religious community' as his vision for it changed (5/29/11). Once he accepted priestly ordination and then episcopal consecration, he

---

[3] Manguso S, *300 Arguments* (Minneapolis: Graywolf Press, 2017), 51.

could see it as 'a network of queer/gay priests— [I have] no big schemes, but something seems to be emerging and I am paying attention' (11/17/15).

Within and beyond the United States, men identified as 'gay' have projected many Christian communities: break-away congregations, small urban circles, secluded monasteries or encampments in the wild. Like Michael's 'network,' some of these projects were linked to 'Old' or independent Catholic lineages. Others claimed very different descent. The resulting history is at once uplifting and sad. Many of the projects fell apart rather quickly. Others began to replay predictable Christian quarrels over governance, styles of worship, and molecules of doctrine. They performed, in willing or unwilling mimicry, familiar churchy vices.

A single example: In August 1970, San Francisco organizers hosted a meeting of the 'North American Conference of Homophile Organizations.' At least, they tried to host it. The meeting was disrupted from its opening session by a 'Radical Caucus,' which punctuated lists of demands with episodes of protest-theatre. One of the liberationists was a 'bishop' who, some witnesses remember, stripped to dance on the head table.[4] His name was Michael Itkin. The following spring, during Easter week of 1971, the same Itkin writes a five-page, single-spaced letter to one of his ecclesiastical subjects, Nicholas Benton. Benton wants to resign from the 'Community of the Love of Christ' and the 'Evangelical Catholic Communion.' Itkin is Abbot of the first and Presiding Bishop of the second. He writes from the 'Hermitage of St. Joseph of Arimathea' on 22nd Street, between Guerrero and Valencia, within San Francisco's Mission district.[5] That year, the neighbourhood already housed notable lesbian and gay institutions. Soon there would be more. In 1975, for example, one block north of Itkin's Hermitage, the basement of a prim Victorian would open as The Catacombs, an

---

[4] Gunnison F, letter to the editor, *Vector* 6, no. 11 (November 1970): 9, 42.
[5] Michael-Francis Itkin to Nicolas S. Benton, letter of April 15, 1971, from a copy in GLBT Historical Society (San Francisco), Raymond Broshears papers (#1996-03), box 3, folder 15. Itkin and Benton led complex lives at the boundaries of queer politics and Christian churches. This single letter can't 'summarize' either of them. It does illustrate some recurring quarrels in gay religion.

S/M sex club. But during Eastertide 1971, The Right Reverend Michael-Francis Itkin, CLC, CHW, chastises a rebellious priest. Benton has broken with him over an old Christian tension, between the claims of a free Spirit sent by Jesus and the institutional authority encoded in victorious notions of 'church.' The tension is inflamed by two issues more particular to gay liberation: Benton demands an overriding commitment to social justice, and he insists on distinguishing the politically enlightened 'gay' man from the mere 'homosexual.'

By way of reply, Itkin does not dance. Instead, he wheels out an ecclesiastical arsenal. He cites church law, Scripture, and dogma—the weightiest of inherited languages. He adopts attitudes of offended piety. He alludes to his prayerful colloquies with God. The bishop also counters Benton's liberationist appeals. Itkin rebuffs the claim that 'the Good News is about these struggles of oppressed peoples' by invoking 'the ontological, transcendent, metaphysical and Inner side of the Gospel ... The Sacramental and Metaphysical side is at least as important as the social struggle' (2). Then, in his last paragraphs, Itkin upstages Benton's liberationist message. He describes his own groups as a *'Jesuene [Jesus-related] Church-Order for the Renewal of the Christ-Mystery, for the Spiritual Renewal of Humanity'* (4). Pushed from italics to capital letters, Itkin declares that 'THE GOAL IS TOTAL HUMAN LIBERATION ... THE SPIRITUAL TRANSFORMATION OF SOCIETY IN THE CHRIST-MYSTERY' (5).

It is worth pausing over Itkin's rhetorical turn. He first casts Benton as another trendy betrayer of Christian truth. Itkin is the True Bishop, the steadfast witness to the Gospel, while Benton is a heretic whose 'itching ears' and disordered desires succumbed to the world's frauds (to recall the model for this rhetoric in 2 Timothy 4:3). Itkin's pleasure in wearing the old titles and pronouncing the old anathemas is palpable, if odd given his activist history. He mobilizes 'traditional' or 'conservative' rhetoric against Benson's political slogans and counter-cultural slang. But the traditional mime falters when Itkin begins to recast the Gospel. He puts on clerical costumes and pious postures only to preach a universal, spiritual *liberation.*

Here is another way into the letter's gyrating rhetoric. Two 'gay' men correspond just as 'gay liberation' gathers steam (all puns on combustion intended). They argue in part about that word, 'gay.' Itkin refuses to treat it as more than a synonym for 'homosexual.' He explicitly denies any claim that 'the Good News is *primarily* about Gay Liberation, Feminism and other liberation struggles.' Yet, in the same paragraphs, Itkin readily identifies himself as an oppressed homosexual: 'our common homosexuality … makes us … common targets of oppression' (2). He keeps 'homosexuality' for his analysis of oppression to block the political reduction he hears in 'gay.' But then he twists around to claim that a higher and better liberation is the heart of the Gospel. What drops out in Itkin's pivots is, of course, any speech about the erotic acts or dispositions supposed to lie underneath homosexuality. Does the 'total human liberation' promised by Itkin's version of 'the Christ-Mystery' leave any room for sex? Or must homosexual loves be hidden once again by golden vestments of silence?

Michael Kelly was rightly critical of the mummery performed by too many pontiffs of gay Christian brotherhoods. He pushed aside 'the ludicrous titles and silly dress-ups' (11/17/15). He also rejected the false either/or. The choices for Christian community aren't limited to the pomp of a legalistic 'metaphysics' or a revolutionary politics of solidarity. Though he would never reduce the Gospel to politics, Michael also never glossed over sex/gender oppression or its continuing toll. What is most important, he insisted, with a holy bluntness, that gay men who seek God from inside homophobic patriarchies must bring their sex with them.

As a bishop, Michael invited me to consider whether I felt called to be ordained by him. The request touched an unhealed wound. Like so many pious young men, I had *of course* tried to discern whether I should test a vocation in vowed community—as a Trappist or Benedictine, Dominican or Jesuit. I visited monasteries and made retreats at a Louisiana novitiate under Spanish moss. Or perhaps I was meant to be a parish priest—if not as a Roman Catholic, then as an Episcopalian. The scatter of possibilities shows how far I was moved by vanity and fantasy, how little by open attention to divine prompting. Decades later, as an Episcopalian married to another man, I undertook a long version of Ignatius's *Spiritual Exercises* across eight months. In one conversation with my director, I mentioned my old struggles over vocation. He replied, 'You made that decision a long time ago. Your ministry is your teaching.'

Michael himself stressed the second point: 'your ministry is right in front of you' (12/20/15). He was not sure about my dismissing the old question. He suggested that my engagement with Roman Catholic religious orders, never abandoned, provided many models for the priestly teacher, even as it prodded me to rethink them. But I feared that ordination would be a sentimental reunion with forms of church power that I had rightly rejected. I did not want to be the child trying to reunite divorced parents in the home that never was.

On the way out of the private labyrinth I had built within Roman Catholicism, I hit upon a test of my intentions. I imagined a papal emissary, in a dandy's flawless suit, appearing outside my door some eerie midnight. He arrives (it would be *he*) to negotiate terms for a truce between Holy Mother Church and gay men. Would I agree to negotiate? Or would I protest that the aim was never to extract a special deal on the side—that such a deal was plainly impossible? Churchly stigmatization of gay men is one aspect of deeper sin that also generates misogyny and gender hierarchy, racial and ethnic subordination, suspicion of all human sex, queasiness before the body of God incarnate. I feared going backwards through a belated ordination—even in an independent Catholic lineage. Or perhaps my allergy to authority consigned me to play the role of Benson, the enthusiastic advocate for unattainable revolutions.

Of course, Michael Kelly wasn't Itkin. The ordination he offered wasn't mummery. He asked me to discern whether I was being called to sacramental and liturgical roles as an extension of my teaching—say, in 'a small circle of ministry, or a home-based eucharistic community' while participating in 'simple, sustainable ways for us all to keep connected as a confraternity' (12/17/15). He described preparing the chrism for ordaining a mutual friend. 'All these gay men of faith, breathing blessing into holy oil for the anointing of another gay man of faith' (12/8/15). He recalled years spent 'encouraging Christian people to take up the bread and wine and 'do this in memory of me'—often they would agree, then turn to me to lead the ritual. Something in us needs priests and shamans' (12/20/15). Certainly, *I* needed them. But did I require that they be licensed by higher (human) authority? Did my scriptural meditations or my encounters with Jesus in prayer suggest that he had come to establish new ranks of priests or new systems of pastoral surveillance? My answer: No. That answer unsettles me.

Our vocations are right in front of us. That insight must apply to our sexual lives as well. Michael's title, *The Erotic Contemplative*, contains the challenge. Heard one way, the phrase is a cliché of Christian mystical traditions. (Centuries before Bernini sculpted Teresa in ambiguous ecstasy, nuns and monks read the erotic poetry of the *Song of Songs* as a hymn to the soul's marriage with God.) Heard another way, 'erotic contemplative' is a paradox underneath our conceptions of how to be church—and how to speak about it. How to be erotic contemplatives *together*?

Sarah Manguso, again: 'In ninth grade I was too afraid to speak to the boy I loved, so I mailed him a black paper heart every week for a year. I wasn't afraid of him: I was afraid of my feeling. It was more powerful than God. If we'd ever spoken it might have burned the whole place down' (15).

My schoolboy anxieties prohibited even the sending of paper hearts. Later, once I had sex with men, the fear began its transfiguration into passion. It was no longer more powerful than God; it was a share in God's life. But it could certainly burn down church buildings—releasing their sacred bodies into open air. I vibrated still with the words, the music, the icons in Christian liturgy. I also joined the rites on gay dance floors, choosing the spot right in front of the thumping bass speakers, the subwoofers.

Michael and I didn't talk much about particular experiences of sex. There was my own reticence and (perhaps) a tacit agreement to avoid sexualizing our friendship. Once he mentioned that he had met someone while sitting on a park bench by the Charles River. He spoke about what took place next as a ministry of hospitality. Pleasure, too, and reconciliation with the bodies we had been taught to despise. But even in sex Michael looked for community. Against the marketing of untethered Gay Titillation or the mind-numbing fables of pornography, sex opens space for generosity, vulnerability, prayers, holy tears—and epiphanies of the divine in our flesh.

There is prayer in the *Sidur* of San Francisco's Congregation Sha'ar Zahav—which is located not many blocks from Michael Itkin's once-upon-a-time 'Hermitage'. The prayer is entitled, 'For Unexpected Intimacy'. Its intention should be committed to memory. 'In the dark, in a strange place, our father Jacob encountered a stranger with whom he grappled all night. He never knew the stranger's name, yet their encounter was a blessing … May this intimate time with another person be an encounter with angels that allows us to both touch and see the Divine.'[6]

When I teach this prayer, I ask the class to consider whether any discomfort arises from a judgment on 'anonymous' encounters or from the very idea of praying over sex. If they can't pray before sex or after it, I suggest, perhaps they should refrain from doing it. No part of a Christian life can lie beyond redemption. I can make the point more abstractly. For too many centuries, Christian theologies of sex banished most of it and then offered tight-lipped excuses for what little remained. No excuses are needed. None should be accepted. Set aside the dour science fictions of eminent theologians to learn *from sex* about divinity.

I opened Michael's message about his cancer on January 29, 2020. I had just finished an online defense at a British university. During it, I had recalled the formalities around Michael's own dissertation. Then, abruptly, this news about emergency surgeries, a terrifying diagnosis, the difficult return to Australia— 'it feels as if I left Australia in late November with one life, and I have come back with quite another.' But Michael didn't stop with that shock. As so often before, he placed his life within larger contexts: the universality of human suffering, the cosmic sweep of Gospel narratives. He recalled the last Mass he attended in New York on the feast of Jesus's baptism. 'I have always loved this feast for this reason—Jesus fully and vulnerably enters into every aspect of our human condition.'

---

[6] Tyler M and Kane L (eds.), *Sidhur Sha'ar Zahav* (San Francisco: CSZ, 2009), 26.

Jesus was executed at a relatively young age by religious authorities and an occupying military. He did not have a 'natural' death—except in the sense that torture and execution are typical of human histories. Michael's choice to walk everywhere with Jesus gave the young rabbi a chance to live the last stages of an aggressive cancer.

During those last months, Michael persevered as he could in the practice of writing. Addressing the community that he had gathered, he taught in new ways about vulnerable bodies on this earth. Our changeable *eros* moves through a body bound by time. Our bodies die. On the way to death, they age. Old age need not disfigure desire, but it does transfigure it. At any age (please remember), you may be asked to hold with absolute hospitality the dying body of a beloved.

In a last 'Letter to Friends,' Michael wrote about looking out on the rural cemetery in which he would be buried. Reading that message, I wondered whether an erotic life mustn't also include our reunion with earth. I responded the same day:

> Michael, I hope that you have many 'good' days left. (Our time, no matter how long or short, only comes to us in days.) I hope too that the days open out sideways into surprising spaces. Whole planets of un-named colours, softest atmospheres. And that you receive epiphanies on them. (5/12/20)

'Epiphanies,' I wrote. Disclosures of the god who takes flesh in a stable. But I also pictured Michael, always bound for Emmaus, catching sight of companions' faces along the way, his new community.

I did not write what I felt most sharply, whether as childish denial or profession of faith: the story wasn't meant to end this way. The words do not stop.

Michael B. Kelly and the Fringe-dwellers Community, Melbourne, circa 1990s: A Personal Reminiscence

Les Cartwright

It was my friend Ivan who first mentioned a new, alternative religious group that embraced the LGBTI community and their friends. The group organized occasional worship and rituals and they were reported to be friendly, inclusive, creative and interesting.

This was confirmed on my first visit one Sunday afternoon at St Stephen's church hall in Richmond. The leader was Michael Kelly, and he called the group *Fringe-dwellers*, meaning folk who were left on the margins by mainstream churches.

Michael warmly greeted each person and made them feel at ease.

He radiated quiet poise and smiled in welcome as he met folk.

I soon discovered that this natural warmth and knack of establishing a rapport were hallmarks of his interpersonal and pastoral ministry.

I participated in many memorable Fringe-dwellers events orchestrated and led by Michael.

Christmas and Easter were especially significant, partly because the rituals were so fresh and alive. There were readings and prayers of course [Noelene, Walter and John B very often assisting], and fabulous music. I'll never forget Geoff's beautiful rendition of *O Holy Night*. The sound and feeling in the words resonate for me today.

One Good Friday, at an outdoor space, we conducted a cleansing ritual with fire and chanting. Pagan in form, but very symbolic.

Another Easter ritual [Holy Thursday] was the washing of the feet.

Compassion, care and inclusion viscerally expressed.

Sometimes liturgical rituals were a prelude to socializing.

One Sunday evening we gathered at the Brigidine Centre in Albert Park.

After the ritual we shared a communal dinner. This was followed by music and dancing, with Noelene and Michael on guitar and

Annie on piano accordion. I remember Michael performed an Irish jig with gusto. Great merriment.

A more reflective occasion was the weekend at Rye when we gathered to contemplate spiritual issues. Study and debate were leavened with beach walks and shared meals.

After four years, the group shifted its regular meeting place from Richmond to Clifton Hill. Rituals continued to be inventive, inclusive and highly collaborative, but the momentum shifted gradually from Fringe-dwellers, a solidarity and support group, to one focussed on advocacy and campaigning: the Rainbow Sash movement.

Here, Michael proved his acumen and fortitude as never before.

I cherish the experience of community with Fringe-dwellers, and Michael's generosity of heart, mind and soul in ministry.

He was a trailblazer with a sharp intellect and love in abundance.

Beyond 'Narcissism': *Ecclesia Peregrinans* and Catholic Homosexual Couples

James B. Nickoloff

I met Michael Bernard Kelly in 2004, appropriately enough at the conclusion of an evening at Spirituality in the Pub in Melbourne. Our common interests were quickly evident: just the year before I had challenged my US Hispanic Catholic theological colleagues to examine a 'queer omission' in their work, namely, attention to real-life sexual experience and its spiritual and theological import. It was a joy to discover in Michael a person who had freed himself from social and ecclesiastical straitjackets and who trusted his mind, heart, and body enough to venture into uncharted, deep, and ultimately life-giving waters. Our exchanges continued over many years and in many places, in person and by phone and email; they always felt like one continuous conversation no matter our respective locations. Our last face-to-face encounter took place on March 17, 2020, at the cafe Waves on the Beach in Frankston—unless you count the Zoom call we had several months later between Miami and Melbourne. Michael's professional focus was simultaneously wider and deeper than mine: theology is the fruit and servant of spirituality, that is, discipleship, and not its parent, guide, or equal. Michael understood this well. Nevertheless, in addition to his passion for beauty and justice, Michael recognized the value of critical thinking and intellectual endeavour, and this made him the ideal conversation partner.

An earlier version of the following essay was presented to the Catholic Theological Society of America in 2011. This version, dedicated to Michael B. Kelly, has been revised in dialogue with his 2007 collection of essays Seduced by Grace.[1] *Re-reading his words now fills me with a selfish sadness as he is no longer available to answer my questions. But it also arouses admiration and, most of all, gratitude.*

---

[1] Kelly MB, *Seduced by Grace: Contemporary Spirituality, Gay Experience, and Christian Faith* (Melbourne: Clouds of Magellan Press, 2007).

In 2021 homosexuality, homosexual persons, and especially homosexual couples—male or female—continue to divide Christian communities as few other matters do.[2] Debate, conflict, and even schism over this issue have erupted in many branches of the Christian family. In the past four decades the Catholic Church, respecting its intellectual tradition, has set forth its teaching on homosexuality with clarity but without coherence or persuasiveness.[3] Most Catholic bishops in the United States apparently believe that the Church's official teaching about homosexually-oriented persons and same-sex relationships—'love the sinner, hate the sin'—is not well understood.[4] It seems more likely that many Catholics—and others—readily comprehend the teaching but do not accept it. Indeed, that teaching has driven countless gay and lesbian Catholics,[5] and many non-homosexual Catholic sympathizers, from

---

[2] Michael Kelly affirmed this in a talk 'Sing a Rainbow: The Challenge of Being Gay and Catholic' given at Melbourne Town Hall on January 30, 2004. ibid., 197.

[3] The inadequacies of the Church's teaching on homosexuality were highlighted at three annual meetings of the Catholic Theological Society of America (in 2000, 2002, and 2004) during panel discussions of the 'Theological Implications of the Church's Teaching on Homosexuality.' Summaries of these discussions may be found in the *Proceedings of the Catholic Theological Society of America* (volumes 55, 57, and 59).

[4] See, for example, United States Conference of Catholic Bishops, 'Ministry to Persons with a Homosexual Inclination: Guidelines for Pastoral Care' USCCB, 2006), which speaks of 'ignorance of the fullness of Church teaching' among Catholics (p. 19) and of the 'special effort [needed] to help persons with a homosexual inclination understand Church teaching' (p. 24). See also pp. 14-15 where the bishops list the 'various obstacles [found in our culture] that make it more difficult for some people to recognize the wisdom contained in [Church] teaching.'

[5] A word about terminology: I agree with Michael Kelly and prefer to use the word 'gay' to designate persons with homosexual desire or what the magisterium usually calls 'inclination'. In scholarly discourse it is common today to reserve the term 'gay' for self-identifying and self-affirming homosexual persons. Here I will add the adjective 'self-affirming', or some other, to the adjective 'gay' to indicate those homosexual persons who are unashamed of their sexuality and who consciously construct a public personal identity which includes their homosexuality. 'Gay' by itself refers to those who experience sexual attraction to persons of the same sex, whether they publicly acknowledge, act on, or even perceive this attraction or not. Thus, it is likely that there have been 'gay' people in all

the Church and makes many who remain uneasy. For decades now we as a Church have been at an impasse, and my reflections here seek to move beyond the present stalemate. Certain particularities of the vantage point from which I reflect are important: I speak here as one whose life and spirituality have been shaped by the Catholic tradition, as a teacher of Catholic theology, and as a married gay man. In 2007 with pride and joy I married my partner of many years, Robert McCleary, in Massachusetts (a marriage now recognized throughout the United States and a growing number of countries around the world).

At the heart of the impasse stand two claims, one psychological and one theological. First, the magisterium of the Church, claiming to be 'expert in humanity,'[6] asserts that same-sex relationships like Robert's and mine are 'intrinsically disordered' and 'self-indulgent,' that is, narcissistic, and thus unable to mediate the love of God.[7] According to the magisterium, there is, by definition, no complementary 'other' in a gay relationship and thus no contact with the divine Other. Far from being holy matrimony, ours is a sinful union because it is said to be a choice *against* self-transcendence which damages the two of us, the Church, and society. Needless to say, our own lived experience calls this into question. Second, in affirming an element of the ancient Christian creed—the Church's

---

human cultures and at all times. How people with homosexual desire respond to their sexuality and construct an identity in their own time and place depends, of course, on the choices available to them. The reason I prefer this usage, aside from its consistency with ordinary (non-scholarly) English, is that I don't find the arguments made in favour of the narrow usage by queer theorists, post-modernists, and/or social constructionists convincing. Most of these scholars are, in the end, forced to do what they claim to oppose in order to speak at all—namely, group persons according to the gender of the object of their sexual desire, whether this desire is acknowledged or not.

[6] Congregation for the Doctrine of the Faith, 'Letter to the Bishops of the Catholic Church on the Collaboration of Men and Women in the Church and in the World' (2004), par. 1. Hereafter, CDF 2004 Letter.

[7] In its official teaching the magisterium nowhere employs the term 'narcissistic' but describes homosexual activity, and therefore relationships, as 'essentially self-indulgent'. The meaning, however, is clear. [See Congregation for the Doctrine of the Faith, 'Letter to the Bishops of the Catholic Church on the Pastoral Care of Homosexual Persons' (1986), pars. 3 and 7]. Hereafter CDF 1986 Letter.

claim to be holy—the magisterium distinguishes between the Church's members who are sinful and the Church itself which is not sinful and cannot be. Once again, the experience of gay people (and many others) challenges the notion of ecclesial holiness pure and simple. Instead, we have learned that while the Church may be an instrument of God's love, it can be, and has been, *at the same time*, a vehicle of sin. How is this possible? How can a holy Church also sin, or even be capable of sinning? How can we logically affirm that ours is not only a 'Church of sinners,' as we officially teach, but also a *sinful Church*, as some have come to believe.[8]

In my view the two assertions—of homosexual narcissism and of ecclesial holiness *tout court*—are both false and, as it happens, turn out to be related. Here I would like to consider their connection in three steps. First, I will take up the magisterium's charge of narcissism, not by recounting how very different Robert and I are (that would take too much time!) but by considering this allegation in light of the long-standing Catholic tradition of 'both/and'—that

---

[8] Karl Rahner began to consider these pointed questions long ago. In 1934 he wrote that 'even though the merely venial sinner remains in [the Mystical Body of Christ] as a living member, yet every venial sin is in a true sense 'a spot and wrinkle' on the Bride of Christ. It is an obstruction to the love of God and as such it is also an obstacle to the free and radiant development in this member of the Church of that love which is poured out by the divine Spirit.' Rahner K, 'The Meaning of Frequent Confession of Devotion,' *Theological Investigations* III, (Baltimore: Helicon, 1967), 187. By 1947 he had concluded that '... it must be conceded that the Church can be sinful in her actions. It goes without saying that this happens in opposition to the impulse of the Spirit and the norms and laws always proclaimed by the Church. But this is surely what is so great about this *faith* in the sinful Church, that she can really do all these things and yet...remain the bride of Christ and the vessel of the Holy Spirit ...' (emphasis in original). Rahner K, 'The Church of Sinners,' *Theological Investigations* III (Baltimore: Helicon, 1967), 261. In 1965 he came to argue that '... the Church cannot be the *subject* of her *own* renewal and purification if she was or is not also in the first place and in a certain sense the subject of sin and guilt' (emphasis in original). This 'certain sense' requires, in Rahner's view, that we see the Church as both a 'free subject' and, following *Lumen gentium* 39, as 'indefectibly holy'. Rahner K, 'The Sinful Church in the Decrees of Vatican II,' *Theological Investigations* VI (Baltimore: Helicon, 1969), 285. He did not, however, offer a conceptual formula for joining the two requirements together.

is, of approaching the complexity of life, especially human life, as both a differentiated oneness *as well as* a complementarity of opposites. Second, I will apply the same lens— 'both/and'—to the issue of ecclesial holiness and argue that because we are an *ecclesia peregrinans* (a Church-on-the-way) we are also an *ecclesia simul sancta et peccatrix* (a simultaneously holy and sinful Church). And third, I wish to consider, very briefly, how moving beyond the claims of homosexual narcissism and one-dimensional ecclesial holiness might lead to a fruitful reconsideration of the concepts of sin and salvation, the very foundations of the Christian tradition, and eventually to reconciliation between the Church's magisterium and Catholic gay couples.

Complementarity and Homo-reality

Liberation movements, multiculturalism, and science have combined in the past half century to make us keenly aware of each individual's and each group's distinctiveness, and understandably suspicious of all generalizations about 'human nature' or 'human being'. At the same time, those who are held in contempt by the socially, culturally, or in the case here, ecclesiastically powerful face the permanent temptation to ignore, hide, or in some way take our distance from the very feature of ourselves which gives offense (sexual orientation, race, gender).[9] Nevertheless, those engaged in the various struggles for liberation have learned that 'silence [about our identities] equals death'.

There is another lesson gay people, like other outcasts, have learned in the struggle for liberation: those who appear so 'other' to the powerful and who indeed are dramatically different in ethnicity, gender, sexual orientation, real power, and/or relative privilege, know that they are also *the same* in fundamental ways. The slogans are well known: 'We are everywhere', 'We are your children', 'I am a man', 'Black is beautiful', 'Gay is good', 'Black lives matter'. These are all ways that the marginalized—or, to be more precise, the

---

[9] Leo Bersani has analysed the 'de-gaying' undertaken by gay men in *Homos* (Cambridge, Massachusetts: Harvard, 1995), at 31-76, especially 32.

despised—have declared a common humanity with their tormentors. Along with other oppressed people, gay people have discovered that nothing causes greater offense than to tell those who despise us that in fact they and we are essentially (I use the term intentionally) the same.

For Christians, the idea of shared humanity is unremarkable; it is the ground of our tradition. All human beings are created in the image and likeness of God. But what happens in practice if we come to believe that the world is built primarily, or even solely, on difference and heterogeneity and lose sight of commonality, sameness, homogeneity? The outcome is clear in recent Catholic teaching on gender: the magisterium asserts that males and females not only differ profoundly from each other biologically but also psychologically and even spiritually. Furthermore, male and female are complementary opposites that will remain so for eternity.[10] But is it true that life emerges only when essential differences are overcome—possible because 'opposites attract', as we gay people are constantly being instructed by Church and society? Or does it also flourish because 'likes attract', as we have discovered for ourselves? Can we not think of the Reign of God as both a unity-in-difference *and* a differentiated oneness? Are sameness *and* difference, continuity *and* rupture, not part of the very fabric of human reality? And what would people whose identity is hybrid say?

While science can today demonstrate a fundamental similitude of reality in ways unavailable to our ancestors, the idea of a shared 'essence' begins early in the Judeo-Christian tradition. In both accounts of the creation of human beings in Genesis (1:26-27 and 2:18-23), but especially in the second one, the common origin of the first human beings is emphasized, not their differences. Today we may find the notion of the woman being fashioned from the rib of the man objectionable, but we cannot deny that the two people find companionship with each other in a way they could not with other

---

[10] CDF 2004 Letter, pars. 8 and 11. This rigid binary view remains unchanged in the 2019 declaration of the Vatican's Congregation for Catholic Education called 'Male and Female He [sic] Created Them: Towards a Path of Dialogue on the Question of Gender Theory in Education' (hereafter CCE 2019 Declaration), pars. 30, 31, 32, 33, and 35.

animals precisely because they are made of the same 'stuff.'[11] Three millennia later the Second Vatican Council continued to speak of the 'single origin' and 'one goal' of humanity.[12] Yet this anthropological '*homo-ousias*,' to put a classical term to a new use, has often been overlooked by readers of the Bible—including the Vatican's Congregation for the Doctrine of the Faith—conditioned as they are to see complementarity and difference as primordial. Consequently, the challenge of the 'homo-mind,' as Leo Bersani calls it, to all ideologies and social arrangements built on what are taken to be irreducible differences, particularly male/female, meets resistance or goes unnoticed.[13] Recognizing sameness relativizes difference; the reverse is of course also true. Needless to say, those who take sameness as seriously as difference are seldom applauded these days, especially in academic circles. Those who think in 'either/or' terms ('You and I are distinct') are inclined to dismiss or even attack 'homo-reality.' Perceiving the fundamental sameness of those whom I've been accustomed to see as radically different is not easy.[14]

Still, a further clarification needs to be made: the assertion of *difference* can, in fact, be either liberating *or* oppressive depending on

---

[11] I thank Robert D. McCleary for helping me to see this point more clearly.

[12] This is most clearly stated in *Nostra Aetate* (Declaration on the Relation of the Church to Non-Christian Religions), par. 1, but the principle grounds much of the theological discussion found in such documents as *Lumen Gentium*, *Dei Verbum*, *Dignitatis Humanae*, *Ad Gentes*, and *Gaudium et Spes*.

[13] 'Homo-reality' and the 'homo-mind' are the objects of theorization by Bersani, op. cit. For an example of the 'hetero-mind' in an otherwise progressive theological work, see Miroslav Volf's *Exclusion and Embrace: A Theological Exploration of Identity, Otherness, and Reconciliation* (Nashville: Abingdon Press, 1996) where difference is still taken as the starting point and reconciliation remains a distant hope.

[14] A glaring example is the unwillingness of the white descendants of Thomas Jefferson to acknowledge their relationship to the descendants of the Black offspring of the author of the Declaration of Independence until DNA proved the link in 1998. We also see the fierce resistance of many to studies that challenge the notion of fundamental differences between males and females or between heterosexual and homosexual persons. The Congregation for the Doctrine of the Faith, for example, decries 'the obscuring of the differences or duality of the sexes'. CDF 2004 Letter, par. 2.

the relative power of those asserting it. For example, when the powerful point to difference ('You are not like us' or 'We are not like you'), it usually serves to oppress those who are 'other.' But when the oppressed do so, it usually liberates by challenging socially constructed boundaries. The same is true of the assertion of *sameness*: claims by the powerful that 'we are all basically alike' (or that 'God loves us all equally') obfuscate real power disparities and actual oppression in the interest of promoting a false reconciliation which leaves injustice intact. However, when those considered 'lesser' claim to be fundamentally the same as those who see themselves as superior, the latter hear a declaration of war and fear for nothing less than the future of civilization. Here, when I assert sameness, I do so from the side of, and on behalf of, those whom Church and society scorn and not in the interest of covering over the real differences that exist among us.[15]

The assertion of *homo-ousias* and 'homo-thinking' does not mean endorsing an irenic approach to oppression in which we attempt to inoculate ourselves against its pain by simply *seeing* things in a new way.[16] As history demonstrates, *beginning* with alterity often means *staying with* alterity, that is, keeping oneself at arm's length from the other.[17] True, those who begin with sameness run the risk of overlooking, or looking away from, differences. Careful analysis, self-education, political organization, and social action in Church

---

[15] M. Shawn Copeland notes that acknowledging difference is risky as it isolates and makes solidarity difficult. However, ignoring difference is likewise dangerous since it leaves inequity in place. See her essay 'Difference as a Category in Critical Theologies for the Liberation of Women' in Elisabeth Schussler Fiorenza and M. Shawn Copeland (eds.), *Feminist Theology in Different Contexts* (Maryknoll, NY: Orbis, 1996), at 145. Copeland sees the interdependence of those who are different from each other as the goal (ibid., 150). While I am proposing an interdependence rooted in commonality and not difference, I second Copeland's warning about the danger of 'indifference to difference'. ibid., 145. What I have in mind instead is what she calls the effort to 'understand what is common and singular and different' (ibid., 144), taking 'common' as fundamental.

[16] This, I fear, is what James Allison attempts in *Faith beyond Resentment: Fragments Catholic and Gay* (New York: Crossroad, 2001).

[17] Copeland notes the 'isolating relativism' that results from beginning with difference and staying with difference. 'Difference', 144.

and society certainly require an openness to conceptual complexity and a desire for solidarity with those who are different. The 'homo-minded' celebrate the humanity shared by all but, at the same time, must train their eyes and ears on oppositions.

Let me return to the contention that same-sex relationships lack complementarity: if we *all* share a fundamental sameness—heterosexual, homosexual, bisexual, and asexual alike[18]-- then no group may be seen as singularly narcissistic. When any one of us stares into the eyes of the person s/he loves, s/he *always* sees someone who is 'like' her or him. And, at the same time, if we are *all unique individuals*, by definition no pair can be self-indulgent. Here, it seems to me, it is time to draw upon the wisdom of the traditional Catholic approach—namely, 'both/and'—as a way to move beyond the limitations of science, as the C.D.F. itself urges.[19] Faith leads us to the rediscovery, as the mystics unfailingly note, that we are *all different* and simultaneously *all the same*.

A Holy *and* Sinful Pilgrim Church

Of the many images of Church employed by the bishops at the Second Vatican Council, that of 'pilgrim' seems the most fruitful to me and perhaps uniquely suited to the reality of 'both/and,' of sameness *and* difference. Far more than 'Body of Christ' or even 'People of God,' the image of 'Pilgrim Church' connotes a dynamic community, one 'on the move' because it has *not yet* reached its destination. It is even more important to recognize that as a pilgrim people the Church remains *imperfect*, urged forward by the grace of God but hindered by the weight of sin. Individual pilgrims are always graced sinners undertaking a journey of conversion. And the same is true of the pilgrim community: in the well-known words of *Lumen gentium* 8, 'While *Christ*, 'holy, innocent and unstained' (see Heb 7:26) knew no sin (see 2 Cor 5:21) and came to expiate only the sins of the people (see Heb 2:17), *the Church*, containing sinners in its own bosom, is *at one and the same time holy and always in need of*

---

[18] I have added to this list those who identify themselves as asexual, an under-recognized, misunderstood, and certainly denigrated group.
[19] CDF 1986 Letter, par. 2.

purification, and it pursues unceasingly penance and renewal' (emphasis added). The distinction between Christ, the sinless head of the Church, and the Body of Christ, the Church, in need of purification is carefully drawn. Even more explicit in this regard is LG 48:

> Already, therefore, the end of the ages has reached us (see 1 Cor 10:11) and the renewal of the world has been irrevocably constituted and is being anticipated in this world in a real sense: for already on earth the Church is adorned with *true though imperfect holiness.* However, until the arrival of the new heavens and the new earth in which justice dwells (see 2 Peter 3:13), *the pilgrim Church in its sacraments and institutions, which belong to this age, carries the figure of this world* which is passing, and it dwells among creatures who groan and till now are in the pains of childbirth and await the revelation of the children of God (see Rom 8:19-22). (Emphasis added.)

The Church's imperfection is further underlined when LG contrasts the Church and Mary: 'While in the most blessed Virgin the Church has already attained the perfection by which it is without stain or wrinkle (see Eph 5:27), the followers of Christ continue to strive by overcoming sin to grow in holiness ...' (no. 65).[20]

The Church has a special gift for memory; indeed, remembering is one of its primary tasks. At the same time, as historians remind us, the Church also has a marked capacity for forgetting, or worse, for covering up, the dark side of our common journey in faith. Pope Benedict XVI is an example of this paradoxical ability: when he opened the Fifth General Conference of the Bishops of Latin

---

[20] Other passages from Vatican II that move in the same direction are found in *Gaudium et spes,* the Council's final word to the Church and the world, which refers to the limitations, imperfections, and even failings of the members of the Church (19, 21, 27-28, 32, 43, and 76). But GS also quotes *Lumen gentium*'s exhortation to Christians to undergo purification and renewal 'so that the sign of Christ may shine more brightly over the face of the Church' (GS 43, quoting LG 15), that is, the ecclesial body as a whole.

America and the Caribbean at Aparecida, Brazil in May 2007, the pope set forth his interpretation of the arrival of European conquerors and the gospel of Jesus in the Western Hemisphere. Recalling 'the great gift of the Christian faith to the peoples of this continent,' he went on to ask,

> Yet what did the acceptance of the Christian faith mean for the nations of Latin America and the Caribbean? For them, it meant knowing and welcoming Christ, the unknown God whom their ancestors were seeking, without realizing it, in their rich religious traditions. [….] [M]oreover, they received the Holy Spirit who came to make their cultures fruitful … In fact, the proclamation of Jesus and of his Gospel *did not at any point involve an alienation of the pre-Columbian cultures, nor was it the imposition of a foreign culture.*[21] (Emphasis added.)

Not an imposition? No alienation? And was the Holy Spirit really absent from the Americas before European colonization? It is hard to take the pope seriously.

Nevertheless, as head of both the Congregation for the Doctrine of the Faith and the International Theological Commission (I.T.C.) from 1981 to 2005, Joseph Ratzinger played a central role in reminding the Church of its chiaroscuro past. By doing so, he joined Pope John Paul II in developing the doctrine of the Church's holiness, something I consider a far-reaching (though perhaps unintentional) theological legacy of the pope. In his words and actions, John Paul II asked forgiveness of Black Africans (traveling to Cameroon in 1985), of the Indigenous peoples of the Americas (in Santo Domingo in 1992), and of Jews (in Jerusalem in 2000) for Christians' shameful participation in the oppression and/or persecution of these peoples.[22] While the pope's words and gestures

---

[21] Pope Benedict XVI, 'Address' (Aparecida, Brazil, 13 May 2007).
[22] The trips themselves were an important statement as the pope could, of course, have issued an apology from St. Peter's in Rome. For his remarks in Cameroon, see *Rencontre du Pape Jean-Paul II avec les Intellectuels et les Étudiants Catholiques* at Yaoundé, August 13, 1985, par. 7. In 1992 the pope undertook 'an act of expiation' and asked forgiveness of the native

were welcomed by many in the Church and beyond, other Catholics have rejected the very notion of apology by the Church, asserting that the Church itself cannot sin[23] and this for two reasons. First, they assert that the Church as a whole is not a *subject* which can

---

population of Latin America and of the Africans imported as slaves (*Message to the Indians of America*, Santo Domingo, October 13, 1992, and *General Audience Discourse* of October 21, 1992). Also in 1992 John Paul II visited the Island of Gorée off the coast of Sénégal, from which countless men, women, and children were deported in chains across the sea. There he spoke of the 'shameful traffic in which baptized persons participated [as they] did not live out their faith'. See John Paul II, *Discours de Sa Sainteté Jean-Paul II à la Communauté Catholique de l'Ile de Gorée dans l'Eglise de Saint Charles Borromée*, 22 February 1992 (my translation from the French). In 2000 the pope travelled to Jerusalem where he declared that 'the Catholic Church … is deeply saddened by the hatred, acts of persecution and displays of anti-Semitism directed against the Jews by Christians at any time and in any place'. See John Paul II, 'Speech at Yad Vashem Museum', March 23, 2000. For its part, the Vatican's International Theological Commission (I.T.C.), then headed by Cardinal Ratzinger, recalled several of John Paul II's apologies in its study 'Memory and Reconciliation: The Church and the Faults of the Past' (1999; hereafter MR). The I.T.C. made special reference to a number of 'faults' for which the Church has asked forgiveness: the division of Christians (both the Great Schism of 1054 and the Reformation), the use of force in the service of the truth, anti-Jewish prejudice, and behaviour by Christians which has encouraged the rise of atheism (MR 5.2-5.5).

[23] The tendency to see the Church as one-sidedly holy arose early in Christian history. By 381 the First Council of Constantinople could speak of believing in 'one, holy, catholic, and apostolic Church', an article not found in the Nicene creed of 325. (Nicaea did not mention the Virgin Mary either.) See Tanner NP, S.J., (ed.), *Decrees of the Ecumenical Councils*, Volume One: Nicaea I to Lateran V (Washington, DC: Georgetown University Press, 1990), 5, 24. By 787 the Second Council of Nicaea justified its view of the Church as holy and 'without blemish or wrinkle' by reference to Ephesians 5:27. This Pauline text, however, clearly asserts that Christ took a *sinful* Church as his bride. He gave himself up for her *in order to make her holy*. Thus, Christ loved the Church *before* it was holy, and since the Church is still growing and still imperfect, Christ is still cleansing the Church he loves so that it '*may be* holy and without blemish' (Eph 5:27; emphasis added). ibid., 133.

freely decide to act.[24] And secondly, they claim that God has promised to protect the Church from falling into error.[25]

In 1984 John Paul addressed an apostolic exhortation to the entire Church called *Reconciliatio et Paenitentia* (On Reconciliation and Penance; hereafter RP) in which he asserted that the Church could only accomplish its purpose of achieving reconciliation in the world by (1) accepting forgiveness from God, (2) undergoing a change of heart, and (3) offering forgiveness to those who have wronged the Church.[26] Strikingly, there was no mention of the Church *accepting* forgiveness *from* those wronged *by* the Church. Yet, clearly the issue of the Church's *ability* to sin is complex. If the Church as such can offer forgiveness, and if the Church as such can mediate God's forgiving love, it would seem to do so by acting as a subject. And if the Church as a free subject can respond to God's grace, then as a free subject the Church must be able to sin by rejecting God's grace.[27]

---

[24] As Francis A. Sullivan, S.J. pointed out, illustrious 20th-century Catholic ecclesiologists from Charles Journet to Yves Congar, O.P. held that a moral or immoral act—such as sinning—cannot be attributed to a collectivity such as the Church. See Sullivan's essay, 'Do the Sins of Its Members Affect the Holiness of the Church?' in Skira JZ and Attridge MS (eds.), *In God's Hands: Essays on the Church and Ecumenism in Honour of Michael A. Fahey, S.J.* (Leuven: University Press, 2006), 251-56. The problem such a view raises, of course, is how the Church can be considered the free subject of grace, and more precisely, the sacrament of salvation, if it is not able to err or to sin.

[25] Nicaea II asserted that Christ promised his holy disciples that he would guard the Church against error, a promise made to future generations of disciples. That Council supports this claim by reference to Christ's promise in Mt 28:20: 'I am with you every day until the consummation of this age.' Nevertheless, it is clear in Matthew's text that Christ promises to 'be with' the disciples as one who *sends* them (the Church) to make disciples by teaching others, through example, to obey. No mention is made of the disciples' own holiness. Rather, Matthew notes the hesitation of 'some' of the eleven apostles to believe and worship the Risen Lord (28:17). Christ's presence to the Church, then, does not necessarily mean that the Church *is* holy, but it does mean that the Church is *called to be* holy. Tanner, op.cit., 133.

[26] RP 11-12.

[27] Karl Rahner went further than Journet and Congar in this regard. As I pointed out above (note 8), he held that '... it must be conceded that the

Though he himself never spoke directly of an *ecclesia peccatrix* but only of a 'Church of sinners,'[28] John Paul's call in RP for a 'fresh ecclesial conversion'[29] became the centrepiece of Catholic plans for the Jubilee Year of 2000.[30] One year before the Jubilee, the International Theological Commission (under the leadership of Cardinal Joseph Ratzinger) went even further than John Paul in laying a foundation for the notion of the Church's sinfulness. In a truly stunning way, the I.T.C. acknowledged the novelty of the Church asking for forgiveness and thus also recognized the possibility of doctrinal evolution. Reflecting on the Church's 700-year Jubilee tradition, the I.T.C. admitted that

> [i]n none of the Jubilees celebrated till now has there been ... an awareness in conscience of any faults in the Church's past, [or] of the need to ask God's pardon for conduct in the recent or remote past. Indeed, in the entire history of the Church there are no precedents for requests for forgiveness by the magisterium for past wrongs.[31]

Church can be sinful in her actions.' Rahner K, 'The Church of Sinners,' *Theological Investigations* Volume III (Baltimore: Helicon, 1967), 261.

[28] The notion of Church as 'perfect society' had already given way at Vatican II to that of 'Church of sinners'. It is true that, in the strict sense, the term *societatis perfecta* refers to the perfect form (structure) of the Church believed to have been established by Christ, and not to its moral status or that of its members. Nevertheless, it is also true that in both the popular imagination and in the mind of the magisterium, the notion came to signify the spiritual purity of the ecclesial body.

[29] RP 13.

[30] The pope pointed out in his 1994 apostolic letter *Tertio Millennio Adveniente* (TMA) that 'it is appropriate that, as the Second Millennium of Christianity draws to a close, the Church should become more fully conscious of the sinfulness of her children, recalling all those times in history when they departed from the spirit of Christ and his gospel and instead ... indulged in ways of thinking and acting which were truly forms of counter-witness and scandal' (TMA 33).

[31] MR1.1. After examining the biblical tradition of admitting guilt for past sins and asking forgiveness of those who were wronged, the I.T.C. concluded (with notable forthrightness) that 'John Paul II's appeal[s] to the Church to mark the Jubilee Year by an admission of guilt for the sufferings and wrongs committed by her sons and daughters in the past ... do not find an exact parallel in the Bible. Nevertheless, they are based on

The fact of a seven-century silence in the face of ecclesial sin may or may not surprise us, but the magisterium's willingness to break with this tradition (lower-case) is notable. This is why it was appropriate for the I.T.C. to speak of 'the doctrinal development of this millennium' and of 'doctrinal development animated by mutual love.'[32] It may be, then, that we are now poised to move beyond the language of 'Church of sinners' to an honest acknowledgement of ourselves as a 'sinful Church.' Because sound theology always *follows* authentic Christian praxis, which is to say, the practice of love, we should be grateful that a changed *practice* in regard to ecclesial sinfulness has preceded further doctrinal evolution ('development') in this area.

But the formulation 'sinful Church' sounds like a simple contradiction and, to most people, like a break with the Church's 2000-year-old self-understanding. However, while this may be true at the level of theological formulation, official or otherwise, history records the repeated re-discovery of what the New Testament itself openly acknowledges. The Church may have been founded on the 'rock' named Peter (Mt 16:18), but Peter and his fellow disciples, after denying Jesus (Jn 18:17), hid from the authorities in order to avoid the same fate as their leader—crucifixion (Jn 20:19). And *as a group* they received the Lord's forgiveness of their betrayal with his gift of the Holy Spirit (Jn 20:19-23). The rock on which the Church was founded was clearly not without impurities.

If the Church is sinful, then ecclesial holiness must refer more to the Church's 'convertibility' than to its 'convertedness'. The pilgrim Church can only be said to be holy when it lives in a dynamic state of openness to conversion which, as we know, involves in a special way the uninvited, the unwelcome, and particularly the despised. *Ecclesial* sin, like individual sin, entails a closing in on the Church itself and a closing out of the other. In short, when the Church as

---

what Sacred Scripture says about the holiness of God, the intergenerational solidarity of God's people, and the sinfulness of the people'. (MR 2.4). The last two points would seem to imply that the People of God—today, the Church—*is* sinful.

[32] MR 5.2. It was referring to the mutual anathemas of 1054 of the Eastern and Western Churches which the Catholic Church annulled at Vatican II.

Church is *open* to conversion, it is holy.[33] It is not hard in this perspective to see the role of those who stand outside, knocking at the gate—such as gay male couples, for example. In closing its collective mind, hands, and heart to those who are 'other,' the Church is surely turning away from the Wholly Other, the Holy One of God who was in fact 'despised and rejected, a man of sorrows, from whom people hide their faces' (Is 53:3-4). By contrast, when the Church opens itself to those whom it has rejected, it may meet its Lord who says, in forgiveness, 'Peace be with you. As the Father has sent me, so I send you' (Jn 20:21).

Sin and Salvation Briefly Re-considered

At present only one married couple has been canonized by the Catholic Church, Saints Louis Martin and Marie Zélie Guérin of France, the parents of St. Thérèse of Lisieux (declared saints by Pope Francis in 2015).[34] If it took two millennia for the Church to honour the holiness of married heterosexual couples, we would be foolish to hold our breath waiting for the Church to give official recognition to the sanctity of the love that can flourish in same-sex couples. Still, as gay people in general and gay couples in particular have discovered, the truth of *homo-ousias* or homo-reality can prevail over what psychologist James Hillman has called the 'fantasy of opposites'[35] when they are willing to be open about themselves and establish friendships with those who view them, and treat them, as 'other.'

But friendships between those who see each other as 'other' are not easy to establish. And perhaps no more Catholic pairing can be

[33] Michael Kelly puts it slightly differently: '[H]oliness is not about being perfect but about being real. [...] The journey into God is a journey into our deepest selves....' *Seduced*, 192. In this he is in complete agreement with Krzysztof Charamsa, the former member of the Congregation for the Doctrine of the Faith who came out of the closet in 2015 and was stripped of his Vatican positions. See his memoir *La prima pietra: Io, prete gay, e la mia ribellione all'ipocrisia della Chiesa* (Milano: Rizzoli Libri, 2016).
[34] Blessed Luigi Beltrame Quattrocchi and Maria Corsini of Italy were beatified in 2001, and their cause awaits a second miracle.
[35] The phrase is used by James Hillman in 'Anima I', *Spring* (1973), 99.

imagined than that of the magisterium and gay male couples. In 2000, even as he called for reconciliation, John Paul II publicly admitted the 'bitterness' he felt as World Pride Day took place in Rome.[36] Aside from all the obvious social, political, psychological, and historical reasons for the estrangement, there are theological minefields which must be negotiated as well. Allow me to conclude by pointing briefly to three questions which gay Catholic couples (among others) put to fundamental Catholic doctrines of sin, salvation, and the cross.[37] In each case the lens of 'both/and,' demanded by gay couples' experience, allows us to see an aspect of the doctrine often obscured in conventional presentations.

First, the doctrine of original sin holds that human beings destroyed their inheritance through 'pride,' the very term chosen by gay people to assert their self-worth. By not respecting their difference from God, our ancestors, we are taught, attempted to make themselves the equals of their Creator. But we all know from historical experience—and gay people often learn this the hard way—that what really distorts our humanity and destroys life on this planet is in fact our unwillingness to be and act more *like God*. We fail not only by *over*estimating ourselves, as the doctrine of original sin asserts, but also by *under*estimating ourselves— 'original humiliation,' we might say. The lament, 'We are only human,' in fact lets us off the hook in aspiring to be like God. Yes, as the Catechism says (no. 396), we must 'freely recognize and respect with trust ... the insurmountable limits' of our creatureliness and our dependence on the Creator. But can 'disobedience toward God and lack of trust in his goodness' (no. 397) not also involve self-repression and lack of self-trust? After the Incarnation, can we ever legitimately use the phrase 'only too human'? I would say that the

---

[36] The pope declared this during his Angelus message on July 9, 2000. In the official English translation, the Italian *amarezza* is translated as 'deep sadness' instead of 'bitterness'—an obvious attempt to soften the pope's statement. See John Paul II, 'Angelus' (9 July 2000), available in both Italian and English at www.vatican.va/holy_father/john_paul_ii/angelus/2000/index.htm.

[37] Michael Kelly pointed out the connection between 'sexuality, the body, pleasure, eroticism, procreation, women, and marriage on the one hand, and holiness, purity, resurrection, and the nature of salvation on the other which developed very early in our history'. *Seduced*, 198.

failure to love the other or oneself (sin) is 'less than human'. It is inhuman. Yes, gay people, like all others, must plead guilty to disobedience and arrogant self-assertion on occasion. But we have also discovered the 'original' sins of ignoring our own reality and humiliating self-negation.

Second, we challenge a standard understanding of salvation found in the Church today. At its heart lies self-transcendence: all avenues to God, the Holy Other, pass through transcendence of self, through relationship with those who are human 'others.'[38] This doctrine makes sense to me, but I must affirm that life with my spouse Robert is a constant experience of living in union with one who is 'other'. (Why does he always put the cereal in the 'wrong' place?) At the same time I cannot help but recognize a profound commonality between us, a sameness that I do not share with women—or with heterosexual men either. In this shared identity— male, homosexual (as well as white, middle class, educated, U.S.- born, etc.)—I find myself at home, not unhappy or unfulfilled, as the C.D.F. declares.[39] Communion, it seems to me, can result from the union of both opposites *and* of likes. It's complicated! In the company of a man, one who is special to me, I find comfort, peace, home. Because of the two-fold nature of the Fall—caused by the refusal to acknowledge God as Other but also by the failure to acknowledge our own likeness to God—salvation means not only being stretched beyond oneself into the world of the other but also finding oneself in the arms of what is familiar. This, I believe, is true for heterosexual couples as well. Furthermore, the Catechism tells me that 'human beings chose themselves over and against God ... and therefore against their own good' (no. 398). But my experience tells me that choosing myself is not always in conflict with choosing God, nor is it always against my own good. In short, salvation seems, not surprisingly, to be as complex as we are. It comes through *both* self-sacrifice *and* self-love, *both* self-denial *and* self-assertion,

---

[38] A clear statement of this is found in CCE 2019 Declaration at par. 33.
[39] CDF 1986 Letter, par. 7. See also Congregation for the Doctrine of the Faith, 'Considerations Regarding Proposals to Give Legal Recognition to Unions between Homosexual Persons' (2003), pars. 4 and 7.

both humility *and* healthy pride. Communion with God is union
with the One Who is wholly other *and* Who became one of us.

Finally, the cross: perhaps it stands as the ultimate symbol of
'both/and' and the way beyond all narcissism—homosexual,
heterosexual, ecclesial. The magisterium is correct, it seems to me, to
speak of a special form of discipleship for gay and lesbian Catholics,
a discipleship which embraces the cross. But the road taken by Jesus
and his disciples is not the way of mute self-loathing nor does it lead
to the cross of silent suffering.[40] Rather, the despised follow Jesus as
he makes his way along a rocky path, meeting lies with the truth,
injustice with denunciation, discouragement with consolation, and
both success and failure with prayer. Disciples see the cross up
ahead, but it is neither the goal of the journey nor Jesus' choice for
himself or for them, as the tradition came to hold and as the
magisterium seems piously to suggest in its counsel to homosexual
Catholics. Instead, the cross represents the price paid by Jesus—or
anyone else—for choosing to be faithful to God, to others, and to
himself.[41] It is the price paid for being open to those who are 'other'
and for recognizing himself in them (cf. Mt 25). The cross is both
an instrument of torture and execution *and* a symbol of faith, of
hope, and of love, a hideous reminder of the consequences of
refusing conversion *and* an invitation to undertake that very
conversion.

Like Sts. Louis and Marie, and like all other couples in the
history of the Church, we gay male couples are *in via*, moving by fits
and starts asymptotically toward the Mystery of God. Yet, perhaps
more than heterosexual Catholic couples, we walk not only in the
gloom of unknowing but also, and even worse, of alienation. 'Alien,'
of course, is alien to God, for no one is 'other' to the God who is

---

[40] Paul Crowley, S.J summed up the magisterium's prescription for gay and
lesbian Catholics in 'Homosexuality and the Counsel of the Cross',
Theological Studies 65 (2004), 519.
[41] Latin American liberation theologians, especially Jon Sobrino, SJ, have
challenged the traditional view of the place of the cross in soteriology. See
Sobrino J, *Jesus the Liberator: A Historical-Theological Reading of Jesus of
Nazareth*, tr. Paul Burns and Francis McDonagh (Maryknoll: NY, Orbis,
1993).

Love and cannot reject. But sinful human beings and sinful churches can and do reject their kinship with fellow pilgrims.

In the end, I take the great Jesuit theologian Karl Rahner as a guide. In 1957, before Vatican II had even been called and as Vatican authorities were scrutinizing his work, Rahner wrote, 'There are things that can only be understood by someone who loves them. The Church is one of these.'[42] But this is true not only *of* the Church but also *for* the Church which can only become the 'expert in humanity' it claims to be by *loving* actual human beings. For followers of Jesus tolerance is not enough. Instruction and preaching are not enough. Only through genuine communion can the Church's magisterium and Catholic homosexual couples move beyond ignorance, fear, and denigration. There is no other way, *Deo gratias*.

---

[42] Rahner K, *Mission and Grace: Essays in Pastoral Theology* Volume 2 (New York: Sheed and Ward, 1964), 106. I thank Richard Lennan for guiding me to Rahner's essay.

'O Captain! My Captain!'

Anthony McAleer

On life's journey you can come across people who inspire or
influence you, or who are important enough to help you get through
a stage in life, or even to become a better human being. In my life
I'm honoured to say I've had some wonderful mentors but one of the
greats was my friend Mick Kelly.

Mick was my Year 10 English teacher at Aquinas College,
Ringwood, but even before I had anything to do with him, he was a
bit of a legend at the school because of one incident. The 1980
annual drama night for the Year 7-10 boys' school was that year a
strange collection of short comedic plays; 'The Mozzies of Wigga
Wigga' and 'Snow White and the Seven Wharfies' were two I
remember, which may give you an idea of the top-quality
productions we had on offer.

Mick, not surprisingly, decided to have his class do something
different; they were going to perform a dramatic scene from 'Lord of
the Flies'. The only problem was, their spot came in about halfway
through the programme, after the audience, made up mainly of
students and parents, had been fed a feast of 'laugh a minute'
offerings, and by then were in no mood for something serious. It
certainly didn't start well when a padded actor in shorts playing
Piggy came on stage to shouts from the audience, 'Nice legs! Shame
about the face!' And it really went downhill from there.

After five minutes of heckling and the students not being able to
deliver their lines, Mick burst on to the stage enraged, and in
defence of his students he screamed at the mob of perpetrators,
calling them 'Bloody shits!' It worked. There was silence from the
'hooligans', and in fact the rest of the audience, including the
suffering parents, for the ensuing performances. But that was Mick,
he'd stand up for you if he thought it was needed and he was willing
to give a voice to the voiceless. It wouldn't be the last time I saw him
defend his students.

Unbeknownst to us until decades later, before we started Year
10, Mick had put in the good fight when the Boys' School principal
decided to separate the Year 10 students into classes based on their

academic ranking. Mick argued that all educational studies discouraged this and that mixing them up actually encouraged some students to progress. He was howled down for his views, so instead he put his hand up to be the home room coordinator for those ranked at the bottom, the group that everyone else thought were the 'hard cases'.

Although we didn't have Mick as our home room coordinator, we did thankfully have him as our English teacher and he was extraordinary. Think of Robin Williams in 'Dead Poets Society' and that was Mick.

He was the first teacher we had who looked upon us as young adults and who treated us almost as intellectual equals. After a lifetime of being in an educational system that looked to control, conform and put you down, to have an adult say, 'call me Mick', instead of 'Mr Kelly', broke some barriers for us.

But to also have an adult open to discuss politics, history and philosophy with you, along with, and in line with, our literary texts that year, helped us to develop. It gave us faith and confidence in ourselves and helped us form our own identity. Mick was the right man at the right time for many of us. With certainty I can look at the group of friends I still have from that class and can recognise his influence and inspiration on us, forty years later.

I know the very first original biographical project I ever wrote was for Mick, a brilliant piece on my grandfather for which he only gave me an 'A minus' – he was a bloody tough marker! I do recall the pride I had in researching and writing that and how I added plenty about my own feelings in there, because 'Mick would want that'. I know that piece gave me the confidence later in life to begin writing historical biographies and in recent decades I have managed to publish 24 books on Australian history and have been awarded an OAM for my efforts. Thank you, Mick, for the first link in that chain.

The year Mick taught us we had a long running battle with the 'teacher' who was our home room coordinator, an insipid little control freak. He ended up hating us so much that he refused to take us on an end of year camp; in fact, we were going to be the only Year 10 class not to have one. However, we did in the end have a camp –

why? Because Mick put his hand up and volunteered to take us – in his own time. Looking back, some of the moments we had on that camp are still legendary – and we owe them to Mick.

As we moved into Year 11, he was still with us and played a large part in creating some great moments in our lives, such as the Central Australia trip and the school musical ('Jesus Christ Superstar' – who would have thought!). Many a musical party was enjoyed by the cast and crew at Mick's house. At the end of that year, he left the college to work elsewhere but by this time, we all considered him a good friend and he remained that way for years to come.

Yet what we didn't know at the time was that he was a gay man who, because of the prejudice of the time, wasn't allowed to identify as that in a Catholic institution because it would have meant his job. Maybe that would have made a difference to us as schoolboys, possibly some giggling behind backs, but by the time he came out we had matured enough to only feel more respect for him for doing so.

We always knew he was a strong man of faith, and we were all very proud when he later went on to lead the Rainbow Sash Movement, confronting Archbishop Pell in his fight for recognition of the LGBTIQ community in the Catholic Church. Watching Pell refusing him communion because he wore the sash and identified as being gay angered us.

By this stage we were very proud of our mate the protest hero – our gay Gandhi.

I know when it came to the Gay Marriage plebiscite, all these straight mates of Mick voted 'yes' – with the thought in the back of our minds – 'this is what Mick would want'.

During his final year he had a terrible time battling cancer, but it also gave many of us the opportunity of spending quality time with him. While living under a dark cloud we still managed to have wonderful conversations we didn't want to end, and many laughs. It didn't take much for us to rally together for this cause – we all knew we owed him more than we could repay.

Thank you for all you gave me and my friends, 'O Captain, my Captain!'

Until my last days I will carry with me my admiration, my appreciation and my friendship for you.

Reverence: A Wide-Open Door – A Response to Michael Bernard Kelly's *Seduced by Grace*

Petrina Barson

1. Experience

I am not a gay man. I'm not even a Catholic. And yet on re-reading Michael Kelly's *Seduced by Grace* recently, my heart burned with the flame of recognition and gratitude. As I read, I felt Michael's seduction at work: that invitation to descend through the layers of my life, through all the daily details and the accretions of the ordinary, to a place of joyful longing that defies description, but which Michael nevertheless eloquently evokes.

Michael uses a variety of words and phrases to describe it: 'the revelation of Divine Love', 'communion with the Other', 'this Absolute Mystery', and simply – 'the Mystery', all of which may sound esoteric or abstract to those not used to mystical language. But the reach of Michael's writing lies in his ability to provide a wider door into the spiritual life than the one offered by institutional religion, to bring onto the same page this spiritual language and the embodied experience of being a human person. For if the reader's soul is not attuned to 'what God is revealing in the mystery of Christ', their body may recognise Michael's description of orgasm:

> In that very moment of ecstasy, in that tasting, that bliss, that knowing, that briefest communion with that which cannot be named, as we are thrown over the peak of consciousness, at the burning 'white hot tip of sexuality', as 'It' shows itself, it withdraws. We are left astonished, filled and shattered by sex, but still we *are* left. (p.9 – all references here are to the 2007 edition)

If the reader is able to relate to this sense of transcendence within their experience of orgasm, then Michael's words have opened a different and more accessible doorway to spiritual experience.

Michael unashamedly sees the spiritual and sexual paths as completely intertwined, even overlain. His message is radical, and dangerous to the institutional church, because of his insistence that the Sacred can be experienced, not despite our embodied-ness, but *through* it. What a scandal to an institution devoted to fencing the spiritual path with dogma, that it could be in our embodied experience, free from assent to any creed, where we encounter God. What a profound antidote to the sexual shame that most people associate with organised religion is the perspective that we might encounter God at the very moment of sexual climax – not as a concept or a set of propositions, but as a direct experience. And what an irony that it requires a gay man, so reviled by his mother church, to take the incarnation seriously, to state the bleeding obvious: if Jesus is the Divine made human, then our embodied experience does not have to separate us from the Divine but can give us access to it.

But Michael's is no call to sexual excess or profanity, despite his comfort with aspects of sexual embodiment normally considered unspeakable. His take on sexuality is vastly different from our culture's usual commodification of sex as simply pleasure or release. Like our spiritual experience, our sexual experience is a longing for communion with the Other, an embodiedness that opens onto divinity. He warns that – like our spiritual path – this opening onto divinity through our sexual natures can be destroyed by clutching or addiction. The very essence of the liminal moment that he discovers in both domains is that it cannot be possessed: 'It' withdraws at the very moment that it seems most complete. To demand that it remain, or return, on our terms, is to distort and perhaps destroy it. And to do so is to fundamentally misunderstand our own nature and the nature of the Mystery itself. Michael writes that

> ... to encounter the Mystery, the Unnameable One, 'God', is
> to go beyond words, concepts, images, and doctrines. It is to
> stand naked, utterly vulnerable in the embrace of the ineffable
> essence of That Which Is, encountering It in ourselves, as
> ourselves, as All. In the immediate withdrawing of the
> Mystery, even as it embraces us, as it licks our lips, we see its
> nature as utterly 'more', ultimately 'beyond', transcending all,

just as in showing we see its immanence, for it is closer to us than we are to ourselves – intimate and immediate in the depths of our humanness. (pp. 9-10)

Here, I think, is a clue to a fundamental underpinning of Michael's spirituality. In every word of this beautiful book there is a deep sense of reverence – for the divine mystery as it expresses itself both beyond and within human being.

Reverence is a word that has slipped from use in daily life, partly, perhaps, because it is mistakenly seen to be the opposite of irreverence – a humorous anti-authority quality that we value. But reverence is not the opposite of irreverence; it is closer to an opposite of arrogance: it is that virtue akin to awe and humility that sees with clear eyes our own smallness in the face of vast mysteries, but also sees those vast mysteries within ourselves. Michael senses that reverence is richly present in the accounts of Jesus' life, as he treads around first century Palestine inviting the powerful and the discarded into an experience of the divine within themselves.

Reverence is owned by no creed. It is at the basis of every moral philosophy and religion that does not tend to dogma and violence. And so, it is potentially a wider doorway through which non-religious people can access the spiritual life. Michael encourages his community to pay reverential attention to their lived experience, because it is a pathway to the divine:

> There is no future in anything but the Truth – the truth of who we are and who we are called to be as fully alive human beings, as gay, lesbian, bi-sexual, transgender lovers imbued with the erotic power of the Risen Christ. This truth is all that really matters in our lives, and the key to it is learning to do what we have been told not to do: to listen deeply to our own experience. (p. 38)

There are many experiences and truths that act as portals to a spiritual life. For some it is an experience of nature that provides glimpses of the Mystery, as we ponder the paradox of our insignificance and interwovenness into a vast universe. In my own life, I think of the experience of birthing my children: of knowing I was participating in a miracle, while also knowing I was its vehicle not its author. I think of mothering, that humbling path of encounter with another being whose life is both completely beyond your grasp and yet – for a time – completely in your hands. I think of my journey to become useful as a doctor, and the many moments when my patients have allowed me to accompany them to their souls' most wounded places.

And yet none of these ordinary experiences are portals to anything more than mundanity, unless they are approached with reverence. Mothering can keep you trapped in the awful detail of life, unable to see the wood for the trees. It can take a moment of stepping back, of looking at my children with 'inside eyes', or a moment of ritual such as a christening or a graduation, to recover a sense of my children's breathtaking beauty and depth. Life as a doctor can feel robotic and exhausting, unless I take a moment to appreciate the miracle of embodied consciousness that is the person sitting across from me.

And here, I think, is a key to understanding why Michael's work and life touch so many, including those who would never identify as religious. Through his writing and his way of being in the world he invites us into an attitude of paying attention to our experience with reverence, with an eye for the mysteries both within and beyond us that are bigger than our egos, our appetites and our understanding. This is not an invitation to simply grasp at ecstatic experiences; rather it is a path through the ordinary, a 'hard work of becoming' through daily acts of service and connection, into glimpses of the extraordinary. And I suggest that it is this practice of paying reverent attention to our embodied experience, of deliberately pausing and cultivating awe, that might be a wide-open door through which we can pass to a mature place where life is richer with colour and love:

> In the midst of this hard work of becoming … there will still
> be tastes and glimpses of that which we seek. These refresh
> us, renew us and encourage us, and they are vital. As the
> years pass, however, these will have a different, deepening
> texture, perhaps quieter, perhaps more free, sometimes more
> searing and overwhelming. Gradually the intimacy and the

ecstasy will become one. Gradually, too, we will begin to
sense a quiet, abiding embrace in the foundation of our soul.
(pp. 17-18)

*

2. Tradition

In my re-reading of *Seduced by Grace*, I have also found that
Michael's emphasis on paying reverent attention to our experience is
only a part of the story. The other part is his insistence on bringing
that experience into dialogue with Christian tradition, and on
reworking and reclaiming that tradition. Michael's reflections on the
story of the woman who lovingly poured fragrant oil over Jesus,
emphasize the sensuality of this act, and Jesus' welcome of the 'erotic
joy of the body'. His beautiful essay 'The Road from Emmaus' places
gay people at the centre of the story, encountering the resurrected
Jesus on the road. These two essays are examples of Michael's refusal
to surrender these gospel stories to the bigots. Inspired by Liberation
Theology, whereby the poor of Latin America interrogated the
Christian gospels through their lived experience, finding solace and
inspiration to critique the church and state from the margins,
Michael sees enough of goodness and Truth in the institutional
church to stay and challenge it.

Michael recalls us to the tradition – but there are problems with
the tradition. Huge problems. And my suggestion is that Michael's
way of understanding and challenging these problems points to the
root of it all: in order for this tradition to be life-giving, it must be
approached and lived with reverence. He suffered for this insight.

His courage and perseverance in continuing to knock at a door
that was repeatedly slammed shut in his face, were remarkable. His
graciousness in continuing to call the Catholic church to be true to
its best self, to embrace the liberating potential in its own sacred
texts, was extraordinary. I'm grateful that I have never had to
demonstrate such fortitude, having made my way many years ago
into a corner of the Protestant church where my unorthodox views

are welcome, even unremarkable. Because, like Michael, I seek to bring my experience into dialogue with an ancient and rich tradition that 'provides a charter for justice, freedom and authentic human values'. (p. 91)

I am grateful for the small community of like-minded people who meet every week to share a ritual centred around the reading and interpreting together of the Christian gospels: mysterious texts whose meanings must be discerned beneath layers of culture; texts that comfort and disturb, that give up their wisdom only insofar as the receiver also unwraps him or herself. Central to those texts are the life and teachings of Jesus, which somehow speak through the gulf of 2000 years, and which remind us still that it is not through our efforts or our cleverness that we discover the Divine, but in emptying ourselves and sitting at Jesus' feet.

The weekly gathering also involves music, silence, spoken prayer, and ritual: actions such as handwashing or candle-lighting that arguably achieve nothing in the 'real' world except a gathering of energy. As we light candles to symbolise our prayer for victims of a natural or man-made calamity, we collectively expand our sense of who 'we' are, reminding each other of our connection to all people, but especially to those who suffer. We encourage one another into action in service of those who suffer, and we make room for our own suffering: for it to be shaped into the language of ritual and held by the little community, and for the light of those ancient texts to be shone through it.

I experience these gatherings, and the broader life of the community, as a kind of cleansing: a washing off of attachment to ego, to material accumulation, to anxiety for the circumstances of my life. And also as a reconnection: to my deepest values, to other people, and to that mystery that is so much bigger than I am and yet one which is present in my innermost world. In other words, I experience them as acts of reverence.

Michael was a friend of that little community years ago, and his presence and perspectives were welcome. But no matter how inclusive and liberal any Christian church is, there is still challenge in Michael's words. Because in this increasingly secularised world, for most people the door of any Christian church is effectively closed to them by the requirements of dogma. Most people cannot access the stories and teachings of Jesus because of the way the church requires assent to doctrine around those teachings before it will invite participation.

Michael's call to begin with our experience, to sense what we can of the Divine within our consciousness and our human connections, is salutary. Because if the Christian Gospel does not first connect with us at the level of experience, then it is bunkum. It is empty words and an ultimately unsatisfying pseudo-intellectual game.

And this should never be so, because the stories of Jesus are profoundly experiential. The Gospels record Jesus' encounters with all sorts of people: from his intervention to stop the stoning of a woman by confronting her would-be executioners with their hypocrisy, to his call to a 'rich young ruler' to give up his treasure to follow Jesus' path, to his furious condemnation of the religious leaders who hid their hardness of heart behind religious orthodoxy. Every word and action of Jesus is an invitation to reverence: to throw off social conditioning to see the God nature in the leper, the blind beggar, the ritually unclean; to tread the humble path of service rather than entitlement; to know both one's smallness in relation to the vastness of God; but also to know that we contain that vastness and are embraced by it.

Where is the Christian denomination, I wonder, whose doors are wide enough open not to fence off the path of reverence with dogma? That recognises that all spiritual wisdom, even the Gospels themselves, are human attempts to name and contain something that defies description? Sadly, it is still a long and often fruitless search to find the one church in a city with enough openness to invite members of the LGBTIQ community – and everyone else – to pay attention to their embodied experience as a source not of shame but of wisdom and insight.

The terrible reality is that LGBTIQ people's experience – in particular – has been unwelcome in the institutional church. It floors me to think that the religion that surrounds the man who fiercely called out hard-heartedness in the religious teachers of his day, could be used to harden the hearts of the religiously minded of our day against people who come – like Michael – seeking 'the tender, gentle, embracing, healing love of Jesus'. (p. 101)

No wonder that the institutional church is in decline. For many, I suspect that it is so much easier, and life-affirming, to abandon the church altogether. There are so many other pathways and traditions that offer language and insights to help us connect with the beautiful mystery and interconnectedness of our lives. Like Michael in *Seduced by Grace* though, I'm not yet ready to move on. There is something about the life of Jesus, and the searing clarity of his ethical teaching, that compels me to stay in his fold. His message of love offered without our needing to earn it, is an antidote to my own hubris, and a profound leveller of peoples.

I believe it is only possible to distort Jesus' message so much if you approach the texts that record his life and teaching without reverence. Without reverence, religious texts become weapons – to exclude, to shame, to dominate. We should remain profoundly suspicious of any religious organisation that substitutes dogma for exploration, legalism for compassion, certainty for mystery. With reverence, those same religious texts become a door: a door through which the Divine might be glimpsed, a door through which even the least religious person might find a connection with their deepest wisdom.

So, for Michael, in the first instance, reverence is not something we learn from religious exploration, it is something we bring to it. And it should be no surprise that for Michael it is the human person, approached with reverence, that is the primary revelation of the divine:

> You are only going to be able to become open to the core reality of the incarnation through profound, intimate communion with other persons. You have got to put your propositions, your doctrines and teachings, aside for a while and engage with persons, engage with them with reverence and open heartedness, in a spirit of justice and love if you are ever to understand even a hint of what God is revealing in the mystery of Christ.
>
> This encounter is going to radically reform all your propositions and doctrines and teachings because they are only ever a stammering attempt to name something which

cannot be named, and they are always in need of reform in the light of justice and love. Once you start to mistake this stammering for the mystery that is being revealed in persons you have moved away from the communion of the Christian revelation. You risk betraying the Gospel itself. (pp. 231-2)

One paradox, then, is that we must bring reverence to our spiritual experience in order for it to be a source of greater reverence rather than of arrogance. And from this follows a second paradox: that for our religious texts and teachings to remain a source of reverence we must set them aside – or at least hold them very lightly – in order to save them. Because to hold them tightly is to risk elevating our 'stammerings' above the embodiment of justice and love that was the person of Jesus. It risks creating partitions of principle: fencing people in or out of the fold rather than standing in appreciation of 'the mystery that is being revealed in human persons'. Surely the point of the teachings of Jesus was to throw open the door to the mysteries of God to all comers who would enter with humility, love, and awe – in other words with reverence.

At Michael's funeral, the order of service bore the words 'born 27 July 1954, born deeper into mystery 14 November 2020'. My sense in rereading *Seduced by Grace* was that my life was enriched by Michael's journey to be birthed more fully into mystery. To dedicate your life to that journey is itself an act of reverence – of walking daily in the knowledge of your own smallness and finitude, and yet of your participation in the vastness of the Divine. It is also an act of 'unknowing', of recognising the limits of what we can understand and subdue with our human intellect, and of opening another channel of knowing – that heart-knowledge of deep connection to values and to 'truth'. Like the walkers on the road to Emmaus, my heart burned within me reading Michael's words, and I remain deeply grateful to him for the way his life opened doors of reverent appreciation of the mystery of what it is to be human in the embrace of the Divine.

Letter to the Editor

Nanette McGregor

Nan McGregor passed away in April 2022 as this book was being prepared for publication. This 'Letter to the Editor' was written in the immediate aftermath of Nan's first Rainbow Sash experience in May 1998, and published in Melbourne's major broadsheet newspaper, The Age, *shortly after.*

Gay son needs mum's love

Although being denied communion at St Patrick's Cathedral on Sunday last was one of the most lacerating experiences of my life – and the hurt and sadness will remain with me until I die – wearing the rainbow sash[1] was my choice.

Had I removed my rainbow sash, Archbishop Pell indicated his willingness to administer Holy Communion to me, but removal of the sash would have been a repudiation not only of my gay son, but of the many decent God-loving gay men, lesbians, their families, siblings and friends within the cathedral.

---

[1] The Rainbow Sash Movement was co-founded by Michael B Kelly and Nicholas Holloway in Melbourne, Australia, in 1997. Its first official action was on Pentecost Sunday 1998 at St Patrick's Cathedral, Melbourne, where 70 supporters wearing the rainbow sash were denied communion. Prior to this action a formal letter had been sent to Pope John Paul II and to the Archbishop of Melbourne, George Pell, informing them of the group's intention. The Core Statement of the RSM reads, 'In wearing the Rainbow Sash we proclaim that we are Gay, Lesbian, Bisexual, Transgender people who embrace and celebrate our sexuality as a Sacred Gift. In wearing the sash, we call the church to honour our wisdom and experience, to enter into public dialogue with us, to work with us for justice and understanding. Together, let us seek a new appreciation of human sexuality in all of its diversity and beauty'. Since its beginnings in 1998, other chapters of the RSM have sprung up in Sydney, Australia, and in a number of major cities in the USA. For more information see: Kelly MB, *Seduced by Grace: Contemporary Spirituality, Gay Experience, and Christian Faith* (Melbourne: Clouds of Magellan Press, 2021).

Our presence within the cathedral was at all times respectful, reverent and dignified. We prayed with the rest of the congregation, some of us even contributing to the collection.

Archbishop Pell's address to the congregation only served to sharpen my awareness of the discrimination all gay people must confront every day.

However, one graceful note was the approach made by two women from the congregation, who apologised to my (straight) daughter, and their declaration that they were not like the archbishop.

In a choice between my gay son and Archbishop Pell's particular brand of Catholicism, I have no regrets about choosing my child.

Had I ever repudiated him, I would have destroyed my family, and would not be fit to be called his mother. From my Catholic parents and Catholic upbringing, I learned more about love and forgiveness than I ever did about hate and discrimination, and for this I am very grateful.

Although I am wounded and offended by Archbishop Pell, the love for and of my family means far more to me than acceptance by a man in ornate vestments.

Of Rainbows and Dinosaurs

Maria Pallotta-Chiarolli

I delivered this speech, at Michael's request, to members and friends of the Rainbow Sash Movement gathered in preparation for an action at St Patrick's Cathedral, Melbourne, in August 2003.

From where I stand here today, looking at all of you, I see rainbows, a diversity of colours, cultures, sexualities, relationships, ways of doing gender, ways of being families. I see the reality of a multicultural, multisexual world. A world of life and love.

This is so different to what's behind me, and to where we're heading soon to protest. Behind me is the grey cold stone of the Cathedral, a relic of the patriarchal past. But its pews are emptying rapidly.

At the risk of sounding ageist and sexist, and being offensive to animals, the Vatican has once again shown that it is made up of old dinosaur-men who seem intent on making the Church extinct, who seem intent on their own extinction. Their statements are made in desperation by a desperate empire that realises that issues around sexual diversity, families and relationships are moving on, and less and less significance is being paid to what the Vatican has to say about them.

But this doesn't mean we can become complacent and hope 'they go away'. We need to be resistant and speak out. We need to ensure that all the good work in shifting social attitudes and reforming legislation, leading to an exponential increase in positive attitudes toward GLBT[1] people over the last ten years, isn't undone by such documents[2], and that politicians like Prime Minister John Howard are restrained from putting them into effect.

---

[1] I have chosen to retain the language and acronyms used at the time of this speech but acknowledge that as our understanding of sexual identity and gender diversity has continued to evolve and expand, so too has our language and terminology.

[2] The document referred to here is 'Considerations Regarding Proposals to give Legal Recognition to Unions between Homosexual Persons' released from the Offices of the Congregation for the Doctrine of the Faith, Vatican,

I'd like to put this document into a wider historical context. So, I hope you don't mind a little history lesson in a cold and rainy park on a Sunday morning. Vatican patriarchal leadership has amassed a long list of injustices and oppressions of various groups: inquisitions, crusades, genocidal colonial missionaries, condoning of slavery, wars promoted or ignored, women oppressed, human life and the joys of living healthily, happily and spiritually, sacrificed for man-made dogma. Yes, much hurt and pain, but also much resistance and resilience, and history has proven how unjust those actions were. History will prove this one is also unjust. We only have to look back at how Catholic women responded to *Humane Vitae* in relation to contraception. That's how our society will increasingly come to respond to, or ignore, this latest attack on another group in society.

If you don't mind, I'd like to also share a little family history. My parents were over from Adelaide the week that this document was released. This latest attempt at collusion between Church and State made them feel appalled, and yet they found it hilarious as well as horrific. They said it took them back to when the Pope and Mussolini signed the Lateran Treaty in the 1920s. This Treaty between the Church and the Fascist State meant that the State would protect the Vatican in return for Vatican support of its Fascist dictatorship and militarism. My parents and grandparents experienced their village being economically devastated and decimated after that Treaty. Subsistence harvests and farm animals were taken away from families, all to feed the Vatican and also the State as part of Italy's feeble attempt at being a colonial power through the war effort. Starvation and sickness were everywhere, peasant farmers were drafted into an army and made to fight a war they didn't believe in. No wonder they cheered when they lost and were quite happy to sit out the rest of the war in prisoner-of-war

---

June 3, 2003. This document echoed the views of certain conservative politicians resistant to the LGBTIQ+ rights campaign and the marriage equality debate, including Prime Minister John Howard in Australia and President George W Bush in the USA. These views were publicly endorsed and enhanced by Archbishop George Pell, who at the time was Archbishop of Sydney following his time as Archbishop of Melbourne 1996-2001. He was elevated to cardinal in 2003.

camps, like my uncle did at Cowra, until they could go home again and set about rebuilding their lives, or starting new lives elsewhere.

My parents recalled how it was well-known that the wealthiest person in the village was the priest and that you had to keep your priest well-fed and regularly report to him your obedience and dedication to both the Vatican and Fascism if you didn't want your village decimated further. But throughout all this, there was resistance. Families hid their food, tried to avoid the draft, sabotaged government and church efforts at enforcing obedience and passivity, and of course the Fascists lost the war.

During those awful years both before and after World War II, girls weren't allowed to attend the one village school, a church-run school, as according to the priest, 'God said' only boys were to be educated. Yet, like many of the girls and women, my grandmother taught herself to read and write from her brothers' books in the evening. Another example of resistance was when the priest declared from the pulpit that girls and women were not allowed to ride bicycles as it meant women had to sit with their legs apart, and 'God said' that was immoral. It was also a concern that girls and women would become more mobile, independent and not so easily controlled in their homes. But what did many of the girls like my mother do? They bribed their brothers for their bikes, went out to the bushes, and learned to ride. Sure, they got sprung now and again and were made to stand at the altar and be publicly shamed as 'immoral sluts'. But that didn't stop them going out there again and riding around the countryside.

Later, most of those 'naughty girls' from that village travelled the world as migrants, setting off on ships for month-long journeys across the world as single young women with very little money and no idea if they'd ever get back to family, but with lots of drive and determination. They raised their own daughters to get good educations and become independent, and encouraged them to speak out, so that some of them like me never shut up. Despite the bans, oppression and public shaming from the Church for being women, they made lives for themselves and passed on knowledge and strategies of resistance and hope.

But they rarely stepped into a church after that, keeping their spirituality as something sacred away from the cold stone and dinosaur roars of the Church. I recall my Mum saying, 'I never actually heard God. God couldn't get a word in what with all the nonsense being said on his behalf'.

We're there again today. I'm sick of old dinosaur men telling me what to do or think or telling me what God thinks. God can't get a word in while all this nonsense is said on God's behalf. But we can still hear and know what God's life-giving rainbow message would be. And we can see it in the positive developments happening in our society.

At a national level, there's been a new Ministerial group organised to look into GLBT health. In Victoria, the Department of Human Services is setting up a research unit for GLBT health.

I'm increasingly asked to go into Catholic schools to work with staff and students on homophobia. I'm increasingly working with parents with GLBT children, such as the wonderful parents from PFLAG, who choose their children over the Church.

I'm also finding that the younger generations are increasingly affirming of sexual and family diversity. I won't even bother defending same-sex families today by spouting stats and research data, as it's so nonsensical to think that being a good parent is dependent on being heterosexual! There's actually quite a lot of data that refutes that connection!

The rainbow-world will keep moving forward in understanding and affirming sexual diversity and family diversity, and the fact that this document has been released is the best evidence of that. If Howard, Bush, the Vatican and the rest of the dinosaurs think this is about the 'survival of the species', history will show that these pronouncements were suicidal and secured their extinction.

Postscript

After a previous Rainbow Sash protest in 1998, I received a letter in the mail. Signed by George Pell, it labelled me a 'dissenter', and declared that 'hereon' I was prohibited from working in a Catholic school.

My first reaction was, 'What's a dissenter?'

Of course, I asked Michael. He and other members of Rainbow Sash explained it, and concluded with, 'Basically, if this was a few hundred years ago, you could be burned at the stake or executed for being a heretic'.

We all agreed that if Pell was around then, he would've very dutifully carried out such a directive in relation to all of us.

Michael was concerned about how I felt receiving this chilling declaration, especially as Pell had demonstrated his supposed efficiency and authority by writing that this prohibition was already lodged in the Catholic Education Office.

I reassured Michael that it sat warmly and peacefully in my heart and spirit, that my family history had unknowingly prepared me for it. Michael nodded and chuckled. He had always respected my refusal of Catholicism and I respected his Catholic faith. And we had long ago found a point of exhilarating connection in our love of Assisi and St Francis!

With a Michael Kelly cheeky knowing smile, he reassured me that it was very unlikely schools would take any notice. They'd just find ways of getting me in to do the work without Pell knowing.

Michael was right. My research with and presentations to Catholic staff and students continued, and indeed increased. Usually, I was the one who raised the letter with school leaders. They would dismiss it and Pell with an eyeroll, a shrug and a smirk. And in 2003, I was still publicly protesting with Rainbow Sash and being invited into Catholic schools.

Strategies of resistance and hope.

Ora Pro Nobis

Benjamin Oh

The eve of the opening of the Australian Catholic Church's Plenary Council, October 2021.

The 24th anniversary of Michael Bernard Kelly being denied Holy Communion, October 1997.

The 35th anniversary of the Vatican's infamous pastoral letter, also called the 'Halloween Letter', published by Joseph Cardinal Ratzinger (later Pope Benedict XVI) on 'The Pastoral Care of Homosexual Persons', October 1986.

This tribute to Michael Bernard Kelly is being written on the anniversaries of these formalised expressions of church institutional homophobia. These anniversaries are a timely reminder of how far we have come as a society in Australia in stamping out violence against LGBTIQ people. They also remind us how far the church still has to go, not just to catch up with successful shifts towards greater social inclusion, but to begin to atone for its perpetration of the sins of heterosexism, transphobia and intersex erasure.

I am blessed to count Michael as a friend and supporter in LGBTIQ Catholic ministry. He was there when things were turbulent and reassured me with his affirmation and Christian solidarity. I give thanks for his life and his Catholic faith. In some ways, he taught me to challenge institutionally conditioned fear and to authentically live in the freedom of faith and love.

As I am writing this, Australian Catholics wanting greater accountability, good governance and meaningful reform in the church are holding their collective breath over the upcoming Plenary Council. The institutional church would have been fortunate to have had Michael Bernard Kelly as counsel amongst the experts and delegates to the Council, charting a way forward for the church.

In October 1997 Michael was publicly denied Holy Communion at Melbourne's St Patrick's Cathedral. Not long after Michael wrote an Opinion piece in *The Age* reminding the church through the

words of the late Cardinal Bernadin of Chicago that 'The Church
must risk authentic dialogue …' with diverse minorities. In that
same article, Michael called for the church hierarchy to, firstly, stop
discrimination and threats regarding the firing of non-heterosexual
church employees, both lay and ordained. Secondly, declare schools
'safe places' so that young gay and lesbian lives are no longer placed
in harm's way in terms of homophobic harassment and vilification.
Thirdly, a 'Year of Listening' be launched where Gay and Lesbian
people are invited to share the truth of their experiences. This, he
argued, should be followed by an ecumenical council 'to examine
sexuality as a whole and homosexuality in particular'.[1] Two decades
later, these concerns are being echoed by the people of God in
Australia through their many submissions to the Plenary Council
calling for justice for their LGBTIQ siblings in and beyond the
church.

Many Catholics have been disheartened by the hierarchical
church's response in addressing outstanding injustices within the
church's modus operandi. Many are hoping that the Plenary Council
will take seriously its obligation to implement all of the
recommendations from the Royal Commission on Institutional
Responses to Child Sexual Abuse whose final report was brought
down in 2017. At the very least the institutional church must address
systemic and long-standing issues such as gender inequality,
LGBTIQ discrimination, racism and failures in church leadership,
accountability and transparency in areas of governance and
organisation.

For some of my Catholic friends, the timing of the Plenary
Council is merely a public relations tactic to deflect the findings of
the Royal Commission – a way to kick the ball down the road. For
many others, it will be nothing short of a miracle if the Plenary
Council produces much more than the predetermined superficial
outcomes set by those hostile to the reforms of Vatican II. As
someone who works supporting and organising LGBTIQ Catholic
ministries, the Plenary Council represents another moment of angst

---

[1] Kelly, MB. 'Selective blessings that sully the faith', *The Age*, Fairfax
Media, November 1997.

at the possibility that the lived experiences and realities of LGBTIQ
Catholics will once again be handled flippantly.

Even after being treated so badly for so long by the institutional
church, LGBTIQ Catholics haven't stopped working for justice for
those who face discrimination in and outside the church. It is sad,
yet also good, that many parts of secular Australia are treating
LGBTIQ people with more dignity and respect than they receive in
their religious spaces. Many more have left the Roman Catholic
Church just so they can preserve their Christian faith. Meanwhile
the church continues to act in unchristian and unjust ways, especially
through the erasure and silencing of LGBTIQ stories, lives and
loves. Who can forget the awful vitriol peddled by the 'No' campaign
in the civil marriage equality campaign, so well oxygenated by some
Australian Catholic bishops?

> 'The real question in all this is not how gay people can dare
> to upset the Eucharistic meal. It is how our brothers and
> sisters can continue to eat at this table when we are refused.'[2]

Michael's question, spoken at the height of the Rainbow Sash
Movement, will continue to haunt us until justice is done, not only
for gay people, but for our siblings who are transgender, bisexual,
lesbian, intersex, non-binary or who share the experience of being
displaced by bigotry and wilful negligence within our churches.

I have a picture of Michael conferring with the Holy Spirit as the
church's Plenary Council gets underway, strategizing new ways of
flourishing for God's Lesbian, Gay, Bisexual, Transgender, Intersex,
Queer children, so that they no longer need to endure the abuse,
erasure, marginalization, discrimination and harm still alive in the
church. Many Australian Catholics will no doubt add their voices to
Michael's prophetic call to the church hierarchy to not only refrain
from pronouncements and behaviours that keep those in the
LGBTIQ community on the margins, but to actively do what is
needed to call them into full and dignified communion.

---

[2] Kelly, MB. 'Rainbow Warriors', *Eureka Street*, Jesuit Media Australia,
September 1998. (This article was a response to a previous editorial piece
by Rev Daniel Madigan S.J.).

'It is not that there is nothing to be done, it is whether we have the will. I remind the Bishops that there are also the 'the sins of omission" refusing to do that which is demanded by love and justice.'[3]

Whether Michael's prophetic call will be heeded by the church hierarchy remains to be seen. It is now 24 years since the church consciously and publicly denied him his baptismal dignity as a gay Catholic.

Australia has a history of rebel saints being denied communion and displaced within the church. Michael is no doubt amongst that holy, peaceful and rebellious people.

So, we beseech you dear Michael, please pray for us.

The Violent Flame of Love: Richard of Saint-Victor and the Mystical Imagination

Constant J. Mews

Of all the students with whom I have had the privilege of working, Michael Kelly was perhaps the most attentive to the mystical imagination. Re-reading his 2014 doctoral thesis, 'Queer Flame of Love: Re-imagining the Christian Mystical Tradition in Light of the Experience of Contemporary Gay Men',[1] of which his principal supervisor was Kate Rigby, I am struck by his remarkable sensitivity and appreciation of the great mystical writers of Christian tradition. When he transformed that thesis into a wonderful monograph, *Christian Mysticism's Queer Flame: Spirituality in the Lives of Contemporary Gay Men*),[2] Michael decided to focus on the contemporary dimension of Christian spirituality, leaving out explicit discussion of the Christian literary tradition (above all, his beloved John of the Cross). Yet I fondly recall our deep and penetrating discussions about many great mystics from the past, with whom he had a profound and empathetic understanding. In the essay that follows, I pay tribute to Michael's contribution to understanding the mystical tradition as a whole. His primary focus was that of his own experience, which he explored through remarkably sensitive presentations of the spiritual journeys of contemporary gay men like himself. Yet what he had to say (and still says through his writing) about the spiritual life more generally, is relevant to all people, whatever their sexual orientation. I offer the subsequent reflection on Richard of Saint-Victor's treatise, *On the Four Degrees of Violent Love*[3] with a sense that Michael would have

---

[1] Kelly MB, 'Queer Flame of Love: Re-imagining the Christian Mystical Tradition in Light of the Experience of Contemporary Gay Men' (Ph.D. thesis Monash University, 2014).
[2] Kelly MB, *Christian Mysticism's Queer Flame: Spirituality in the Lives of Contemporary Gay Men* (New York: Routledge, 2018).
[3] Richard of Saint-Victor, *De quatuor gradibus violentae caritatis*, in Ives, *Épître à Séverin sur la charité. Richard de Saint-Victor, Les quatres degrés de la violente charité*, ed. Gervais Dumeige (Paris: Vrin, 1955), 89-177.

been enormously interested in what this twelfth-century author had to say. An English translation by Andrew B. Kraebel of this relatively short text is included within an anthology of Victorine writings about love.[4] While I would love to be able to continue that conversation with Michael in the present, I shall endeavour to pick out themes in which he would have been interested. He was aware that authors from a past age can still have a lot to say for the present, even if much has evolved in the way we understand identity.

Michael had a profound interest in the theme of spiritual awakening as involving recognition of one's sexual identity. For him the issue of coming out as gay had a spiritual significance comparable to the initial stage of spiritual awakening to which so many authors refer. Yet he was also painfully aware of the corrosive psychological damage that could be done by ecclesiastical assumptions, both explicit and implicit, that anything to do with sexual identity was the work of the devil. For that reason, he was attracted to mystics, like John of the Cross, who were (like himself) gifted writers, deeply marked by their experience of the dark night of the soul and what Underhill called 'the purgative way'. In particular, Michael was fascinated by the way the Song of Songs functioned within Christian tradition by providing a much more erotic way of talking about the spiritual life than either scholastic philosophical theology or the apocalyptic thundering of the prophets. Richard of Saint-Victor's *Four Degrees of Violent Love* captures a sensibility that Michael made particularly his own, that the spiritual life was not necessarily comfortable and that it could well involve challenging social convention.

Richard (d. 1173), reportedly of Scottish ancestry, came to Paris to join the single-sex community of Augustinian canons at the abbey of Saint-Victor, probably sometime in the 1140s, although it could have been earlier.[5] Unlike monks, Augustinian canons did not live a strictly enclosed life. Their way of life, defined by the Rule of Augustine, involved both a contemplative and an active dimension.

---

[4] Feiss H, *On Love. A Selection of Works of Hugh, Adam, Achard, Richard and Godfrey of St Victor* (Turnhout: Brepols, 2011), 263-311.
[5] Coulter DM, *Per Invisibilia ad Invisibilia. Theological Method in Richard of St. Victor (d. 1173)* (Turnhout: Brepols, 2006), 246-8.

Whereas Bernard of Clairvaux (1090-1153) spent most of his life in a monastic community remote from any major city, Richard opted for a different kind of religious life, defined by combining pastoral involvement and contemplative ideals. He was certainly familiar with the writings of Hugh of Saint-Victor (d. 1141), the first great teacher at his abbey. While Hugh certainly had a mystical dimension to his teaching, his major reputation was that of a theologian, who produced perhaps the first major systematic synthesis of Christian doctrine, *On the Sacraments of the Christian Faith.*[6] Richard was certainly capable of expounding doctrinal matters, producing a major treatise *On the Trinity* that went into major detail about the relationships between the Father, Son, and Holy Spirit as divine persons generated by the dynamism of love. Richard's major fascination, however, was not with doctrine as such, but the stages of the spiritual life. He was a prolific author, becoming most well-known for two major works on the spiritual life, *On the Twelve Patriarchs* (also known as *Benjamin minor*) and *On the Ark of Moses* (also known as *Benjamin major*).[7] His method was to focus on biblical figures not as historical personages, but as emblems of the life of contemplation and action, with particular emphasis on the role of experience in shaping the spiritual life. This emphasis on experience is where Richard's vision of the spiritual life connects to Michael Kelly's analysis of gay Christians. While discourse about sexual identity in the twenty-first century is very different from that of the twelfth century, in both periods we find a fascination with the concept of experience—not to replace doctrinal understanding, but to provide a new framework from which ideas were generated.

Richard probably wrote *On the Four Degrees of Violent Love* c. 1170, towards the end of his life.[8] Here, he abandons his earlier technique of using Biblical figures to personify types of spiritual life,

---

[6] Hugh of Saint-Victor, *On the Sacraments of the Christian Faith*, trans. R. Deferrari (Cambridge, MA: Medieval Academy of America, 1951).

[7] Richard of Saint-Victor, *Richard of Saint-Victor: The Twelve Patriarchs, the Mystical Ark and Book Three of the Trinity*, trans. Grover Zinn (New York: Paulist Press, 1979).

[8] Kraebel, in his introduction to Richard of Saint-Victor in Feiss H, *On Love. A Selection of Works of Hugh, Adam, Achard, Richard and Godfrey of St Victor* (Turnhout: Brepols, 2011), 263.

and instead focuses solely on the language of the Song of Songs, above all the verse 2:5, as rendered in the Old Latin, *Vulnerata caritate ego sum* (I have been wounded by love), perhaps even more dramatic than the dreamy version offered by Jerome in his translation of the same verse: *quia amore langueo* (because I languish with love). The verse had often been mentioned briefly by various Church Fathers, but generally without any detailed commentary. Even Bernard of Clairvaux, who broke with exegetical tradition by recovering Origen's interpretation of the bride in the Song of Songs as meaning the individual soul as much as the Church, avoids detailed reference to the Old Latin translation of this verse only and relies on Jerome's translation (about languishing with love) within Sermon 51 of his epic series of homilies on the Song of Songs.[9] Richard's originality was to interpret the verse 2:5 (in the Old Latin version) about being wounded by love as a focus for reflection on the nature of love as violent and thus continually challenging our identity.

Richard's boldness is to use throughout his treatise the word *caritas* interchangeably with two other Latin terms for love, *amor* and *dilectio*. This linguistic range makes it very difficult for any English translation to convey the full rhetorical impact of this short treatise. Augustine had tended to use the word *caritas* (a translation of the Greek *agape*) for selfless love, as embodied within the divine nature in the mutual love of God the Father and the Son, from whom was generated the Holy Spirit. He preferred to use *amor* in the classical sense of the Roman poets, to mean a fleeting passion that tended to be physical rather than spiritual, with *dilectio* reserved for love between friends, without a sexual component. Bernard of Clairvaux, inspired by his engagement with Origen's commentary on the Song of Songs, had transformed exegetical tradition by combining these different terms (*caritas*, *dilectio* and *amo*) to create a more dynamic sense of love between the soul and the Word of God.[10] Yet while

---

[9] Bernard of Clairvaux, *Selected Works*, trans. Gillian Evans (New York: Paulist Press, 1987), 1971-80.
[10] See Mews CJ, 'Bernard of Clairvaux and Richard of Saint-Victor on the Pursuit of Ecstasy and the Development of a Mystical Theology', in Posa C (ed.), *A Not So Unexciting Life. Essays In Honor of Michael Casey, OCSO*

Richard certainly absorbed Bernard's focus on experience in the spiritual life, it is striking that he did not become a Cistercian monk. Richard's desire to join the community at Saint-Victor suggests that he wanted to carve out a new spiritual identity, one which combined the active and contemplative life (of Martha and Mary) within the life of an urban-based Augustinian canon, rather than within the monastery, as imagined by Bernard of Clairvaux. Richard's understanding of the stages of love extends the concerns of Bernard of Clairvaux with the process of loving, as laid out in *On Loving God* (*De Deo diligendo*) but presents the spiritual life as an anguished rather than ordered journey of the soul.[11]

Richard is unashamedly affective in how he speaks about the first stage of being wounded by love: 'He is ablaze with desire; he seethes with feeling. He boils and pants, groaning deeply and drawing long, deep breaths.'[12] The second stage, one of binding, is no less difficult: 'it burns the mind with ceaseless fire and enkindles it with the continuous boiling of its desire.'[13] It is a state of being involved externally as well as internally: 'In the second degree a man can still be occupied by outside business in his actions, but not in his thoughts, since he cannot forget what he loves. ... The third degree exists when the mind can know nothing but its desire, while the fourth, which is also the last, exists when not even the very thing which the mind desires is able to satisfy it.'[14] The absence of any reference to intellect in this process of development is striking. Richard is concerned to affirm the fundamentally affective nature of the self. In the 1150s, a Cistercian monk, Isaac of Stella (d. 1169), had formulated a much more intellectualised vision of human development, inspired by comments of Boethius in his *Consolation of Philosophy* in his *De anima* (On the Soul), addressed to his friend,

(Collegeville, Minnesota: Liturgical Press, 2017), 157-87 and Mews CJ, 'Intoxication and the Song of Songs: Bernard of Clairvaux and the Rediscovery of Origen in the Twelfth Century', in Nagy P and Cohen N (eds.), *The Medieval Book of Pleasure* (Turnhout: Brepols, 2017), 261-74.
[11] Bernard of Clairvaux, *Selected Works*, trans. Gillian Evans (New York: Paulist Press, 1987), 1971-80.
[12] Feiss H, *On Love. A Selection of Works of Hugh, Adam, Achard, Richard and Godfrey of St Victor* (Turnhout: Brepols, 2011), 277.
[13] ibid., 278.
[14] ibid., 279, 282.

Alcher of Clairvaux.[15] Isaac theorized that the spirit could ascend from sensory knowledge, through the senses, imagination, and reason, and rising to the realm of intellect, climaxing in spiritual intelligence. Isaac's formulation in his *De anima* was influentially taken over by the author (Alcher of Clairvaux?) of the *De spiritu et anima*, a treatise widely circulated in the thirteenth century under the name of Augustine.[16] In the *Four Degrees of Violent Love*, Richard explicitly mentions this distinction between intellect and understanding (*intellectus* and *intelligentia*): 'The Lord indeed kindles emotion, but he does not yet illumine the intellect. He inflames desire, but he does not yet illumine the intelligence. And so, in this state, the soul is able to perceive its beloved, but, as has been said, it is not able to see him.'[17] Richard's phraseology suggests that in this treatise he is consciously criticising the more intellectual model of understanding, inspired by Boethius, promoted by Isaac of Stella.

In the *Four Degrees*, Richard provides a series of analogies to spiritual growth, always emphasizing the place of emotion. Unlike Bernard, he draws on the human experience of the marriage bed, without commenting on whether partners are male or female: 'We know that in human emotions marital love (*amor*) ought to hold the first place, and, therefore, in the marriage bed that degree of love (*amoris*) that is accustomed to being master over all other feelings can be good.' Richard is concerned, not with theorizing the process of knowledge, but with theorizing desire: 'Often we are drawn toward loving something by our feelings, and yet we are restrained by our reason. And often we love many things by deliberate choice, though we do not strive after them desirously.'[18] Richard likes sexual

---

[15] Isaac of Stella (1974), *De anima* in McGinn B (ed.), *Three Treatises on Man: A Cistercian Anthropology* (Spencer, MA: Cistercian Publications, 1974).

[16] See Isaac of Stella (1974), *De anima* in McGinn B (ed.), *Three Treatises on Man: A Cistercian Anthropology* (Spencer, MA: Cistercian Publications, 1974) and Mews C 'The Early Diffusion of the *De spiritu et anima* and Cistercian reflection on the Powers of the Soul', *Viator* 49, 2019, 297-330.

[17] Feiss H, *On Love. A Selection of Works of Hugh, Adam, Achard, Richard and Godfrey of St Victor* (Turnhout: Brepols, 2011), 289.

[18] ibid., 285.

imagery: 'In the first degree the beloved is visited frequently, in the second she is married, in the third she couples with her beloved, and in the fourth she is pregnant.'[19]

Perhaps the most remarkable feature of Richard's reflection on the violence of love relates to the fourth and final degree. For Bernard of Clairvaux, the fourth and final stage of loving God is defined by the soul loving oneself for the sake of God. For Richard, there is a consciously social dimension to this final stage: 'And so those men who are able to lay down their life for their friends reach the highest height of love and now are placed in the fourth degree of love; now they fulfill the apostolic injunction: 'Be imitators of God just like the dearest children, and walk in love just as Christ also loved you and surrendered himself for you, sweetly-scented offering and sacrificial victim to God (Eph. 5:1-2).' This final injunction to imitate Christ in humility stands in sharp contrast to what he too often observes in this world: 'Behold into what great boldness of pious presumption the consummation of love often raises the mind of a man; behold how it makes a man dare to be more than a man.'[20] While the soul might cross in the third stage to God, the fourth stage of violent love leads to descending to humanity with patient endurance. Richard's final line summarizes his vision: 'In the first it is led back, the second it is carried over, in the third it is transfigured, and in the fourth it is reawakened.'[21]

Richard of Saint-Victor has nothing to say specifically about gay spirituality, a category whose potential importance has been well argued by Michael Kelly in the conclusion to his monograph.[22] Nonetheless, Kelly is part of a very long-established tradition that crosses the centuries. In his perspective the spiritual life is a process of continual awakenings, as each of us comes to terms with our identity. Richard's understanding of the spiritual life is not the same as that of Thomas Aquinas, who in the thirteenth century was interested in his perspectives but preferred a more intellectual version

---

[19] ibid., 286.
[20] ibid., 295-6.
[21] ibid., 296.
[22] Kelly MB, *Christian Mysticism's Queer Flame: Spirituality in the Lives of Contemporary Gay Men* (New York: Routledge, 2018).

of the contemplative ideal.[23] Michael Kelly would take this perspective a step further, by arguing that we must explicitly acknowledge our sexual identity as part of any spiritual awakening.

---

[23] Hart K, *Contemplation and Kingdom. Aquinas reads Richard of St. Victor* (South Bend, IN: St. Augustine's Press, 2020).

Touching Skin: An Elegy for Michael Bernard Kelly

Christian Scharen

'What is touch–: not the touch not the hand but the white heat it floats through.'

Natalie Diaz, Ink-Light, from *Postcolonial Love Poem*

I walked up from the subway into the cold winter air. Pulling out my phone, I texted Michael. In New York for a short visit in late 2019, we met at Rockefeller Center to take in the holiday spirit of the giant Christmas tree and the revellers ice skating on the rink below. He texted back saying he arrived early and was in St. Patrick's Cathedral, praying in the quiet cavernous space. I laughed, thinking he's trying to avoid the bustling crowds moving up and down 5th Avenue past Saks famous holiday window displays and, across the street, the line waiting to get into the LEGO store. I briefly wondered what a complicated space St. Patrick's, the Roman Catholic Cathedral of New York, must be for him given his life-long work protesting the church's rejection of his personhood as a gay man. Yet always welcoming complexity, I do believe he genuinely experienced it as a sanctuary, a space for him, too, to pray. Suddenly, I saw him on the corner in his cute flat cap, flashing his impish grin. I threw my arms around him, and he, me, in a tender embrace. In that completely Michael way, he sighed audibly, and held the hug much longer than the typical male chest bump and hand on the back thump. I smiled, knowing this friend through my skin, through my body, as much as by the recognition my eyes offered. We found a coffee shop, and with steaming cups of tea (of course, tea!) sat down to catch up on each other's lives. Little did we know the gravity of the situation to unfold for him in the next weeks and months.

That December feels like a lifetime ago. As I write in mid-July of 2021, it is hot and humid in New York City. The 'feels like' temperature and the humidity are both in the 90s most days, turning me into a pool of sweat even before I descend into the hell of the subway station on my commute to work. So, it makes me smile re-reading Michael's piece about our July together in New York in 2017 and his 'temptation to complain about the intensely hot and humid summer.'[1] I'd been living in New York for five years by then, working at a progressive seminary on the Upper West Side. I'd always loved New York, but now to actually be at home in the city thrilled me. Among many joys in my seminary role, each summer I hosted a month-long research seminar on some topic related to religion and social justice. That summer with Michael, the seminar focused on 'Reformations: Past, Present, and Future' that marked the 500th anniversary of the Protestant Reformation sparked in 1517 when an unknown monk named Martin Luther posted 95 theses for debate on the church door in Wittenberg, Germany.

We gathered similar risk-takers, change-makers, scholarly rabble-rousers. The seminar offered participating fellows a spaciousness for research and writing. Yet as important, it offered a daily seminar in which each fellow shared their work, and the flow of conversation rippled into evening over drinks and dinner. Michael was in the midst of finishing what would become *Christian Mysticism's Queer Flame: Spirituality in the Lives of Contemporary Gay Men*. Having this summer together recalled for me our first meeting in the mid-1990s as he worked on the video series, *The Erotic Contemplative*, almost like I had a front row seat for bookend moments in his long, brilliant career as a public theologian. In this essay, I sketch some of what I know about skin, the body, and Christian faith as a result of this friendship of nearly 30 years.

*

In objective terms, skin is a soft outer covering of tissue serving three central purposes: protection, regulation, and sensation. Part of the integumentary system, it is a mammal's largest organ, and, arguably, its most important. Sometimes, the word 'flesh' is used as an

---

[1] Michael Kelly, Greetings from New York. bentstreet.net, 2017. https://bentstreet.net/greetings-from-new-york-by-michael-bernard-kelly/, accessed July 13, 2021. Also reprinted in Kelly MB, *Seduced by Grace: Contemporary Spirituality, Gay Experience, and Christian Faith* (Melbourne: Clouds of Magellan Press, 2021).

equivalent, although technically it pertains to the soft substance—
muscle and fat—found between the skin and bones. So central is
skin to human well-being that studies show lack of touch in infants
inhibits brain development and stunts social and behavioural
abilities, and in the most severe cases can lead to death.[2] Touching
skin in humans releases oxytocin and vasopressin from the pituitary
gland, and their combined effect has been dubbed a 'biological
metaphor for social attachment', and intimately related to physical
attraction, love, and sexuality.[3] Some touch causes harm, to be sure.
But to touch, skin to skin, with consent and kindness is, in short, to
give life.

Perhaps as much as anyone in my life, Michael taught me this
truth, that touch is life-giving, and one more: that such touch is
holy. That touch is holy should not be a shocking claim to Christian
ears. It should not, but too often is. It should not: Christianity is a
religious tradition centred on the claim that God became flesh and
dwelt among us.[4] The claim that God becomes human in Jesus
eventually developed into the doctrine of the incarnation, a term
whose literal meaning makes the point: in/carne, or in/flesh. Not
just in his identity, but in his ministry, too, flesh, skin, touch is
crucial. Interestingly, it is not only in Jesus' touching, but also in his
being touched, that healing occurs. The woman in Mark 5 had bled
for twelve long years and expended her resources in fruitless efforts
to find a cure. Yet in her boldness, she touched Jesus and was made
well.[5]

Too often Christianity became a religious tradition that
embraced what the philosopher Charles Taylor calls 'excarnation,'
effectively turning a religion of incarnation into a body-phobic, sex-
phobic shadow of what its founder set in motion.[6] The reasons for

---

[2] Harmon K, 'How Important is Physical Contact with Your Infant?'
Scientific American (May 6, 2010), accessed July 5, 2021.
https://www.scientificamerican.com/article/infant-touch/.
[3] Carter CS, 'The Oxytocin-Vasopressin Pathway in the Context of Love and
Fear,' in *Frontiers in Endocrinology*. (December 22, 2017), accessed July 5,
2021. https://www.ncbi.nlm.nih.gov/pmc/articles/PMC5743651/.
[4] Gospel of John 1:14.
[5] Gospel of Mark 5:24b-34.
[6] Taylor C, *A Secular Age* (Cambridge: Harvard University Press, 2008), 554.

Christianity's transformation away from its incarnational roots are many, and far beyond the scope of this piece. Yet the rending asunder of this central Christian truth was something Michael fought against his whole life. His final major work, *Christian Mysticism's Queer Flame*, makes a strong case that 'renewal, wisdom, and inspiration are sorely needed in a world, and a church, in which body and soul, sex and spirit, earth and heaven have been so tragically split apart'.[7] While acknowledging this is not his main thread of argument, his deeply prophetic and integrative vision saw that this deformation of Christianity has profound consequences not only for people, but for life on this planet. 'The exploitation and abuse of the earth and her creatures are not unrelated to the long-standing, religiously sanctioned suspicion and denigration of all that is corporeal, material, sensual, and sexual in our human selves.'[8] His clear articulation of the wider stakes of his arguments shows both the ambition and the generative, integrative scope of Michael's work.

It is interesting, then, to read Michael writing about 'the saintliness demanded by the present moment,' drawing upon the 20th century mystic Simone Weil. He quotes her statement that 'Today it is not nearly enough merely to be a saint, but we must have the saintliness demanded by the present moment'.[9] With a deep humility, he outlines the implications of her argument with an acknowledgement that those gay men whose stories he tells are such examples of saintliness. He writes,

> She is calling for a new, creative, daring incarnation of holiness—something so unexpected that it will require holy genius. This genius will bring forth a new synthesis, a new integration, a new dawning of radically open-hearted sanctity that embraces the insight and anguish of the contemporary world, that draws from the deep wisdom of the past, and that

---

[7] Kelly MB, *Christian Mysticism's Queer Flame: Spirituality in the Lives of Contemporary Gay Men.* (New York: Routledge), X.
[8] ibid., 3.
[9] ibid., 1.

midwifes transforming grace with its irrepressible vision of a
future filled with justice and peace.[10]

Yet 'a new synthesis, a new integration, a new dawning of radically
open-hearted sanctity' could hardly be found in more robust form
than in the person of Michael Kelly. He exuded it and inspired it in
others. When I met Michael, I'd been on a journey of
transformation from my rural western childhood where I'd done
everything I could to avoid being targeted as a 'fag' simply because of
my chubby body and my too-large-to-get-away-with-it breasts. It's
illogical, to think of it now, and cruel besides, but the harassment I
experienced taught me to sacrifice for a harder body, to play football
but not join the debate team, and formed me in fundamental
assumptions about acceptable bodies and pleasures. In the two years
before moving to Berkeley for graduate school, I'd both met two
dear gay men, both religious leaders, who broke open my
assumptions and forced a reconsideration of my childhood views,
and I'd married my college sweetheart. In seminary, I began a
research project studying the Lutheran church's construction of anti-
gay theology and policy and trying to find within the tradition
sources of affirmation for, as I'd put it today, an affirming theology
grounded in desire, consent, and pleasure. That, I wanted to say, was
God's posture towards us: that we might know ourselves to be
desired and experience the pleasure of that desire through the touch
of another with the strong moral protection of mutual consent.

*

Michael was a tremor; no, better, a full-on earthquake entering my
life at this time of rethinking and growth. Two scenes, decades
apart, stay with me.

I walked up the winding tree-lined road in the Berkeley hills, my
mind lost in the intricacies of Alexander Irwin's stunning rethinking
of the classic theology of love that for most of the twentieth century
had held pride of place with a pure, divine agape over the sullied and
oh-so-human eros. I'd read the famous work by 20th century

---

[10] ibid.

Swedish theologian Anders Nygren, *Agape and Eros*,[11] and felt an intuitive sense that, as Queen Gertrude says in Shakespeare's Hamlet, 'The [gentleman] doth protest too much, methinks.'[12] In a too-simple take, Nygren opposes the two forms of love, and makes agape the noble form, the Godly posture to which we are called in Christ. The Lutheran emphasis on our inability to reach God, but instead, in faith, receiving God who reaches towards us in Christ, seemed to me to discount the very way we are created by God for desire, of each other, of the world, and ultimately, of God. If, as Luther's sacramental theology puts it, 'Christ fills the earth like wheat fills a sack,' could not all those delights we encounter—from the flapped open petal of a purple iris, to the tender embrace of a sleepy child, to the honeyed bliss of a lover's lips—open a way to know God and God's desire for us?[13] Irwin draws on another 20th century European theologian, Paul Tillich, to argue for a quite different, and to me, more sensible role for eros as a means by which we come to know ourselves as meant for loving and being loved. In this view, eros works together with, or better, alongside of agape, rather than as its antithesis. Tillich has a very troubling personal history in his life—abuse of his professorial position for sexual misconduct with students, a fact Irwin addresses openly. Nonetheless his careful study joins, as he puts it, a major and ongoing 'reappraisal of eros … in progressive theological circles.'[14] Yet, as I soon came to realize, such a revolution of thought does not produce new habits of bodily experience.

In the early 1990s, Michael was living in a house with some religious brothers he worked with at St. Mary's College, a Christian Brothers school in near-by Oakland. I arrived at the house, wandered down the path to the door, and knocked. The door

---

[11] Nygren A, *Agape and Eros*, trans. Philip Watson (Louisville, KY: Westminster Press, 1953).
[12] Shakespeare W, *Hamlet*, edited by G. R. Hibbard. The Oxford Shakespeare. (Oxford: Oxford University Press, 1987), 3.2.216.
[13] Luther M, 'The Sacrament of the Body and Blood of Christ—against the Fanatics', trans. Frederick C. Ahrens, in *Luther's Works, American Edition*, vol. 36 (Philadelphia: Fortress, 1959), 343.
[14] Irwin AC, *Eros Towards the World: Paul Tillich and the Theology of the Erotic* (Minneapolis: Fortress Press, 1992), ix.

opened to a barefoot Michael, wearing what looked to be yogi pants and a loose, long-sleeved V-neck white shirt. He gestured me into an open living room with ample couches in a large L shape. We had just met the previous year through my student pastorate in a Danville congregation on the other side of the Berkeley hills. Danville is a toney suburb with a faux-Mexican building code ensuring every building, including the church, looks the same. It would be an unlikely setting to run across someone like Michael, save that the pastor, Steve Harms, a renegade who broke away from the conservative Missouri Synod Lutherans during their 1970s fundamentalist take-over, was just as likely to be barefoot and wearing yogi pants. The story of how he ended up in Danville is one more proof for me of the surprising nature of God's ways in the world.

We sat on the couch on that particular afternoon sipping, as would become our habit, a cup of strong black tea. I shared about my reading and reflection, and some of what it led me to think in terms of the erotic as a much wider and more important presence than the Western reduction of it to merely the genital, or even to the sexual. He wondered aloud if I had ever considered the erotics of touch, and of the skin as our largest sexual organ. Skin, he remarked, is immensely sensitive, and because of that sensing ability, some places where there is a concentration of nerve endings an intensity of pleasure is possible. He matter-of-factly noted this is why the penis and clitoris are the source of such ecstasy when touched, but then, taking me completely off guard, said the anus has nearly the same concentration of nerve endings. Had I ever explored that as a centre of pleasure? With some chagrin on my part, I admitted I had not. In his kind, pastoral, yet always direct way, he said 'I'm aware this may make you uncomfortable to speak about directly, but, well, what are you waiting for? You don't need to be gay, or even have a partner, to explore your own body, its responses and pleasures!' He laughed, seeing my visible shock, and yet I welcomed the challenge and permission his comments embodied. We talked some about the connection between our bodies being created good, and the exploration of the body, of the skin. Such exploration, he suggested, can be seen as an exploration of God whose creative genius shows itself just here, in the spectacular possibilities for knowing oneself as deserving of pleasure and joy. It is as if we were made for knowing ourselves as erotic creatures—it is literally part of our very anatomy and physiology. My tea finished, and my world blown open, I wandered back down the hill to my little apartment.

Many years later, in New York city for the summer research seminar, I met Michael for dinner in Harlem. He was dealing with a lot of exhaustion. The seminar's program of afternoon seminars with dinner was about the limit of his energy for the day. I tried hard to give him space, and at the same time, I wanted to have a deeper conversation. After a week or so of settling and getting into rhythms, we met at a classic Harlem restaurant, the Red Rooster, landing a sweet sidewalk table on a beautiful July evening. Over wine and a meal of the sort waiters dislike because it is the length of two ordinary dining parties, and the requisite tips, we caught up on our lives. There was a frailty about him I didn't know what to do with, and at the same time, an intensity, a kind of clarity of purpose. I was married before we met, and our long-running joke was if I ever got divorced, he'd get first dibs for me. As I shared with him the challenging story of my marital troubles, a twinkle appeared in his eye, as if he couldn't help himself, and he said, 'Chris, my chance may have finally come,' and we both broke out laughing.

As the conversation turned to his life, he noted that increasingly he found himself alone, and although fine with that for the most part, he so much longed to be held. I touched his arm, and our hands found each other as his voice softened. The truth is, he said, what a baby needs, we continue to need our whole life through. I shared with him that I felt so moved by the Anglican queer priest and theologian Jeffrey John who wrote about the Genesis creation stories not as a male-female binary undergirding heterosexual complementarianism and procreation, but rather a depiction of human loneliness and the deep desire for companionship, something shared alike by people of all gender and sexual identities.[15]

*

---

[15] John J, 'Permanent, Faithful, Stable,' Christian Same Sex Partnerships (London: Darton, Longman & Todd, 2000), 20.

My phone still has a string of texts from December 2019 and January 2020 from Michael. It is painful to read. 'It's been tough. Initial diagnosis is colon cancer.' Many planned dates for connection with Michael had to be put off because of the subsequent hospitalization and illness. Yet, finally, before he departed for home, we shared dinner in his hotel apartment. I planned to bring mild miso soup, and he asked me to bring enough for Noelene, who'd arrived to care for him. I said, 'Of course!' And then this text: 'I'm also wondering if you'd be up for bringing a pie or half a pie. My sister tries to find something sweet for me each day as dessert—and I have very fond memories of your pies!' It was January, but I found fresh blueberries and made my favourite fruit pie, a whole one. Our last time together, full of tenderness, full of wondering about the unknown, yet yearning still for the sweetness possible in this life, and tasting it, touching it, feeling the pleasure of it. In the end, Michael taught me this: whatever there is that is sorrowful, painful, and gut-wrenching in this broken world, we can reach out to each other and insist on finding something sweet each day. It may be the ecstasy of intertwined bodies; it may be the heady joy of camaraderie, an arm-in-arm for a social justice protest; or it may be the simple touch of fingers on an arm, or the delicious explosion of deep blue berries on the tongue.

Rainbows Against the Wreckage

Greg Curran

'One night in my twenties I watched a red-face-drunk – the spitting image of Vinnie O'Connor, but full-grown now and twice as lethal – chase two men down Boylston Street for holding hands. He roared that he would shred their faces with the broken bottle he wielded. How much of that did he learn in church, along with his catechism dose of 'intrinsic evil'?' (Paul Monette, *Becoming a Man*, 1992:36)

We gather beforehand

Light mist is falling on the almost deserted Fitzroy Gardens. It is a beautifully still morning as we gather. What brought me here I wonder? The thought has gone over and over in my mind as I've wandered up and down the autumnal paths, kicking the leaves, ridding myself of the residues of frustration, anger, emotion.

To step inside that cathedral today is to face the past, to face that place where I first learnt rejection. To wear this sash is to deliberately mark myself an outsider, but 'outsider' status has been a part of me since I was a teenager and even before.

> As a teenager I knelt before my god, in what I was told was a place of peace, a place of sanctuary.
> I prayed for the daily torment, the constant exclusion and moments of physical abuse to end.
> My prayers were never answered.

I look across the incredibly vibrant greens of the grass, the drops of moisture delicately poised upon each blade – life is brimming within these gardens. I look away, towards the cathedral complex, and all I can think of is death and rejection.

We gather behind a building in the gardens. It buttresses us from full view of St Patrick's. Just its spire rises in the distance, coldly elegant in the clear morning air.

Laid over the railing near where we stand are the
rainbow sashes we will soon wear, the colours
radiating from them, dazzling in these wintry gardens.

I look around me to the mums standing in for their gay and lesbian
children, children who can't bear to risk exclusion once more. I look
to those determined to stand honestly within the church,
proclaiming who they truly are. I stand with them, believing in their
rightful place at the communion table, even though I no longer wish
to receive communion myself.

There is a sense of calm as we join arms in a small circle, this
physical symbol of support and unity.

But the years of a church telling me I'm a sinner, disordered,
with a tendency towards evil, begin to turn over in my mind.

We proceed to the Cathedral

A fence spans the cathedral.

Why do we need a fence around a cathedral?

As we near the gates I feel numb. Tears are already welling.

Security guards stand near the steps of the main door.

What will I say if they stop me from going in?
Am I doing anything that would create suspicion?

Do I look too weird?
What about my hair? I've got it arranged in
clumps of spikes. Yep, it's my hair that'll do it.

I check myself. Why this sense of guilt? Why this fear, as I step –
uncensured as it turns out – into this cathedral?

I think of the rainbow sash in my pocket. If I wore it unfurled
across my shoulder, would my entry be assured? Would I pass
through unnoticed?

We scatter throughout the Cathedral

We sit in small groups of twos and threes, linked with others for support.

> With these people I feel valid, accepted.
> With them I feel I have the right to be here and to fully
> participate.

> > My eyes zero in on the words of the Mass
> > Program: 'Welcome to St Patrick's Cathedral'. It's
> > the first of many ironies.

They process in

Slowly they move down the aisle. Oh, so 'dignified'. The young choir boys, the altar servers, candle bearers, the processional cross, deacons, clergy. The mitred one, crosier in hand.

> Confected 'solemnity'.

Sit back and enjoy the performance but be warned, it's an all-male cast!

The Choirs sing

Their voices, oh so 'beautiful', like 'angels'.
> I imagine the beatings such a voice could earn you.
> The taunts it could earn you.
> > And yet here it signatures the institution.
> > Like men in long gowns.

The 'King' sits on his throne

The mitred one proceeds to his episcopal 'throne'.

> Episcopal coat of arms positioned above him on the stone colonnade of the sanctuary.

Attendants on low seats each side. Subtle wafts of the medieval monarch.

Not so subtle later, in his homily. His subject – fathers and sons – speaks directly to the 'wayward' ones.

Fathers should assert authority and provide discipline in the household. Sons want their fathers to say 'no' to them!

The Mass begins

We reach for our sashes. Trembling hands in pockets and handbags. Breathing shifts. Heart rate rises. Air pushed from lungs. The material of many colours goes over my head and across my shoulder.

I am marked. We are marked.

Anonymous we were acceptable. Now, rainbow sashed, unworthy. But unworthy to whom?

Across the cathedral splashes of colour – colour against the uniform browns and greys.

These rainbow colours have come to mean so much. Colours of life.

But not here. Here they brand the wearers defective, unfit. Deficient for the 'body of Christ'.

But who are they to decide?

My heart, my spirit, remembers this. Bewildered child. Tainted. Unwelcome.

We sit together in that row

But strangely welcomed, too. Within this small space, on a heated cathedral pew, with other rainbow sash wearers each side.

Being church within a church. Shoulder to shoulder. My right to be here, to participate as my fully, sexual self.

But this sense is fleeting, fragile. A pocket of warmth within the enormous cavern of the cathedral.

I grasp Maria's hand. Maria, who is beside me. As the shadow of the past looms and shudders, her hand anchors me, reminds me I am whole and loved, connects me to a world outside this one.

We offer each other a Sign of Peace

We extend our hands and hugs to one another. Vivid life. Touch. Warmth. The only human point in the Mass. Sanctioned but controlled.

Cautious, we reach out to those around us. Will our rainbowed selves be accepted? Will people refuse my offered hand?

But my hand is received. And other hands reach out. Smiles met with smiles. Peace exchanged. Acknowledgement shared. It is what community can be.

It is what must not be forgotten against the starkness of what is to come.

They seek communion

I watch them moving up the aisle, risking this most ultimate rejection.

The mitred one holds the ciborium. He who decides who is worthy – or not.

My eyes are drawn to him. Expressionless. Face of stone.

Outstretched hands of rainbow sash wearers are left empty. Their rights, dismissed.

A blessing is offered in place of bread. An inconvenient blessing. Begrudging. Face-saving. Coldly designed to keep the line moving.

One after the other they move forward, offering themselves, asking to receive.

One after the other they return to their seats. Numb. Tearful. Walking the lonely journey, again.

As I watch, my heart pounds. Memory written in the body. Body of pain. Body of shame. The daily grind of exclusion. What to make of the body of Christ?

Maria comes back to the seat, our eyes connect, tears falling. The shock on her face, the incredible sadness.

My hand becomes one with hers, it's all I can do. And in doing so a source of power, an incredible bond, an energy lifeline, runs through us. Is this what they fear?

In connection we become whole once more.

When Bill returns to his seat next to me, I see the same look of devastation. I reach for his hand, too. He grips it so, so tightly.

In the aftershock, our hands enmeshed, our bodies close, connection is all. One body!

Prayer time after communion

In the aftershock, I can't keep it in. All those years of struggle. Up they come. I can't hold them down.

As I cry, I fight for restraint. What will be let loose if I lose control now?

And she's there once more. Maria. We hug. I hold so tightly, wanting this moment to go on.

> Let this hug erase the turned backs, the comments hurled,
> the ingested notions of 'shame', 'guilt' and 'sin'.
> Let this hug erase the schoolyard graffiti, the head smashed into the locker.
> Let this hug erase the people stepping over me as I lay concussed …

Mass concludes

The parade of males processing from the altar nears us. The head usher raises his hand, as though motioning traffic.

Down the centre of the cathedral they go, the altar servers and candle bearers and deacons. The mitred one, the crosiered one. Shepherd of his exclusive flock. And then they exit left, to the sacristy. Performance over.

People stand, collect their things, leave slowly via the main door. Our rainbow sashes seem to float on that moving sea of humanity.

Outside we join together (once more)

Outside the Cathedral gates.

The rain has cleared now, a little sunlight peeks through. Upon the damp autumn leaves we lay flowers, resting against the cold iron fence. A wreath is placed above, hung over the spikes of the fence.

Arms wrapped around each other – we bring to mind those gay and lesbian students in Catholic schools now.

> We remember those who've survived Catholic education, the Catholic system, the dogma, the hierarchy.

> We remember those who didn't make it, couldn't make it through.

> The suicides, the attempted suicides, the self-persecution, the beatings, the abuse – the silent wreckage of young Catholic lives.

> I look across to him, the mitred one, standing now on the cathedral steps, king of his domain. Performing again. Cameras. Journalists. Providing his ten second grabs for the bullies and bigots.

> Only here, outside the gates, arms, voices, smiles and tears. This is life.

We're on the news

I see myself on the news. I can hardly recognise myself. The haunted look of times past. Alive, revived, potent. There, on my face.

I open the door to my unit, to my space. The relief is overwhelming.

> The array of posters on the wall, the books scattered over the floor, on the desk, the familiar images all around. Here is home. Home.

I've made it through.

> Simon comes down the stairs anxious to hear what has
> happened. I wrap my arms around him feeling his body, his
> warmth, connection.
>
> As the tears begin to well I softly murmur, 'Where do I
> start?'

An Appreciation of the Life of my Dear Friend, Michael Kelly

Bernard J. Lynch

Teach us to number our days aright that we may gain wisdom of heart.

So the Psalmist says in Psalm 90.

If I were to sum up the life of the one we celebrate and mourn it would be, 'Wisdom of heart.' Not simply the wisdom of the knower – although Michael had much knowledge – but the wisdom of the lover. And time is on the side of those who love. Only those who love can touch the meaning of time, which in its profoundest significance is always a time of meeting, of encounter, of being with another, of shared and received presence. Yes, in his life Michael touched the meaning of time because there was much love in his life.

First of all, Michael loved life. For him, to breathe, simply to be, was itself a grand and glorious thing. He knew that life itself, existence itself, was the most precious thing we know. Life is grace to us: our own lives and the lives of those around us. All things great and small are gifts: the treasure that we can at any moment discover, the banquet to which we are all equally invited. For Michael, the true value of all that exists was discovered in the unique way in which one values a gift. He cherished life and existence and especially other people, and so enabled and inspired them to discover the treasure hidden in their own lives. He looked on all things with the glad eye of the lover.

There was the warm intimate love of his home and family. His love of his friends. His love of those of us who shared his journey of theological reflection throughout the world. I can truthfully say that love was given a primary place in his heart and in his dwelling place. He was in the best sense of the word a homemaker, because he was first of all a life giver and love maker – and at times a pain bearer. The message he passed onto us was a message of love. However powerless you feel, however bare of miracle solutions, you can touch another person. You may even move an acre of God's world if you will only reach out very simply, in love. In the words of C. Day Lewis, he knew:

Self-hood begins with walking away
And love is proved in the letting go.

Yes, there was much love in Michael's life, and yet his life was
touched ultimately by divine passion. First, the love of God; the
conviction that he was loved by God, with a love beyond all telling.
He believed, although like all of us he did not always understand,
that the love of God was our ultimate environment. He intuited the
dictum of Dante that it is God's love that moves the sun and other
stars and holds all things together. Not fooled by the sometimes
shallowness of religion, its injustices and arrogance, he was graced to
see beyond this. His religion was life affirming and liberating. His
God was a loving God who knew the tears of things, a Mother God
in every sense of the word. As the marvellous English mystic Julian
of Norwich puts it, 'As truly as God is our Father, so truly is God
our Mother'. He especially wanted us free from institutional religion
so that we could be friends of God.

Yes, time is on the side of those who love. And yet, how little
time there is for any of us. There is so much to be done, so many
need our love, and there is so little time. I cannot promise myself
tomorrow. Only today. Only today am I alive to live and to love. Oh
yes, a resurrection beckons beyond and today's Gospel guarantees.
But tomorrow's resurrection will not raise today's world from
despair, will not feed this hungry stomach. We cannot wait for
tomorrow, for tomorrow the other may be dead. And in the wisdom
of his heart Michael knew the importance of the now in human
living: not that each moment should be a frantic search for God and
goodness, for holiness in Word and work; that way madness lies.
Simply a simple awareness that God and his images are here and
now; in this suffering, in this joy, in this person. Today is important,
for salvation is now; love is now; life is now; God is now.

Finally, I turn to speak of the sorrow in our hearts, especially the
sorrow of Michael's family and friends. It is his physical presence
that we will mostly miss. His presence to us and our presence to
him. This involves both the comfort of a comfortable presence and
the challenge of an unfinished relationship. The mourner longs not
only for the accustomed communion with the one now dead, but

also for the opportunity to redress a wrong, complete a service or fulfil or redeem the relationship. To pray for and to the dead is to lend one's personal concern and vital energies in some way to the completion of the essential life-commitment of the dead. It may in particular cases even be the concrete fulfilment of this through the change it makes in the living.

Prayer for the dead reaches into the unknown mystery with hope rather than meandering inconclusively around it. In the actual practice of prayer for the dead, we come to realise that it does not bring Michael back to the earthly life he has left behind. No! In prayer for the dead, we come to know in our heart of hearts that the one whom we 'have loved long since and lost awhile,' belongs to Christ in God. After his journey to the 'far country' he has entered his eternal home – with his loved ones who have gone before him – and found a peace, which passes understanding. Little more can be said. We are indeed on holy ground. To paraphrase the poet W.B. Yeats:[1]

> Rich memories, nothing but memories
> But in the grave all, all, shall be renewed
> The certainty that we shall see this man
> Leaning or standing or walking
> As in the first loveliness of his youth
> And with the burning fervour of his youthful eyes
> Has left us muttering like fools

'Air dheis De go raibh an ainm.' May God's light shine on his soul.

'Ni bheidh a leitheid ann aris.' His equal will not be seen again.

Thank you, Michael, my fellow priest; fellow activist; and life-long friend.

London, Candlemas 2021

---

[1] Yeats WB, 'Broken Dreams'; *The Wild Swans at Coole, and other poems* (New York: The Macmillan Company, 1919).

Queering kingdom politics

Marcus O'Donnell

The Erotic Contemplative: Reflections on the Spiritual Journey of the Gay/Lesbian Christian, a series of lectures delivered by Michael Kelly, was originally recorded in 1994, released 1995 by Erospirit Research Institute, and relaunched digitally in 2020. An edited transcript of the original video series published by Clouds of Magellan Press was launched in December 2021 at the Harehole in Fitzroy by Marcus O'Donnell. Below are his remarks and observations.

It's a great pleasure for me to be here today to honour Michael, to celebrate his life and to celebrate the publication of *The Erotic Contemplative* in its third incarnation.

In the Zen tradition they talk about 'transmission', which is when a disciple has absorbed the tradition and made it their own and a teacher can say to them, your mind and my mind are one mind, you too have earned the right to teach others. It occurs in a public ritual that recognises the new teacher. But in reality, it is not a single moment, it is a continuous practice that is forever networking seekers together in a tradition which is always drawing on its history and always becoming new.

There are many Zen traditions. Chan took early Indian Buddhist teachings and transformed them into a new Chinese tradition. The Japanese then took Chan and transformed it into Japanese Zen. Zen teachers then travelled all over the world and today we see Indigenous Zen traditions with their own rituals and insights in many countries including Australia. My own Zen teacher Roshi Susan Murphy will often move from reflecting on an ancient Chan story to insights she has learned from Aboriginal Elders and then to her own unique experience as an Australian woman who was shaped by 70s feminism.

Christianity, and certainly Catholicism, has a more fractious relationship to the development of independent traditions within its history and tends to excise rather than celebrate the formation of new voices in its network.

So, it takes remarkable courage to dare to speak from a truly independent place in the Catholic tradition like Michael did in 1994 when he recorded *The Erotic Contemplative* lectures. He claimed his own authority to speak, no one had given him that authority. Given Michael's history as an activist with Rainbow Sash it is tempting to read this as a work of dissent, his electronic nailing of his thesis to a cyber church door. But this is not a work of dissent. This is an insider's view of the tradition which is also richly overlaid with Michael's lived experience as a gay man. Michael speaks as someone *totally inside* this tradition but someone free enough to make it his own.

And so I think there is also something of the Zen Master in Michael as well as the Christian mystic.

As most of you probably know, The Erotic Contemplative lectures were recorded in 1994 and distributed from 1995 as video tapes by Dr Joseph Kramer in his *Sex Wisdom Series*. They more recently had a second outing as YouTube videos and now they have a third outing in book form. So, in welcoming this new edition of *The Erotic Contemplative* I want to begin by taking you back to 1994 when in September that year Michael sat down in California to record these lectures.

What was the moment that Michael was speaking to when he recorded these lectures? What was it like to be lesbian, gay, trans, queer in 1994?

It was the year that we celebrated Stonewall 25, so it was a significant moment in LGBTI history. In Australia it was 16 years after the first Mardi Gras, we were midway through the Keating Labor government which, right at the time Michael was sitting down to record these lectures in California, was just about to introduce a bill to expunge Tasmania's Sodomy Laws – the last remaining sodomy laws in Australia. The government was forced to do this because the United Nations Human Rights Committee had ruled we were in contravention of the International Treaty of Human Rights. This was due to the long fight by Nick Tonnen and his then partner Rodney Croome, who had fought for this all the way to the UN. In Melbourne, a month before Michael recorded these lectures, we saw the infamous Tasty raid where 460 queer party goers were strip-searched by very over-zealous police searching for drugs, something even then-Premier Jeff Kennett agreed was 'disturbing and extreme'.

So even though we were well into the era of gay liberation things were still fragile.

AIDS was still killing gay men even though drugs were beginning to emerge as a treatment. In fact deaths from AIDS continued to increase; in 1995 HIV became the leading killer not just of gay men but of all Americans between 25-44.

HIV was very much in my mind at that time. I tested positive in 1993 and in 1994 I had what I call my first mid-life crisis and took myself off to art school. At the end of that year I was lucky enough to participate in 'Don't Leave Me This Way' at the National Gallery in Canberra the first large AIDS Exhibition at any national gallery anywhere in the world. It was curated by Ted Gott who is now part of the NGV team, and who early next year will bring us another pathbreaking show: 'Queer', which will include 400 artworks from antiquity to the present day.

Radical queer politics was still a force. ACTUP was still a vibrant movement. In New York Rudi Giuliani had just become Mayor and they put him on notice from day one and their protests followed him throughout his Mayoralty. And it was the second year of the Clinton presidency – and he had just backed down on his election promise to end discrimination against lesbians and gays in the military, giving birth to the Don't Ask Don't Tell compromise. Something that took 17 years to undo. It was the year that Nelson Mandela becomes president of a new South Africa and their post-apartheid constitution explicitly recognises sexual orientation in their bill of rights which outlawed discrimination.

It was also a time of rich gay and lesbian storytelling, that included mainstream successes and joyous experiments.

In 1993 Tony Kushner received the Pulitzer prize for the first part of his extraordinary *Angels In America* and Jeanette Winterson released her wonderful *Written on the Body*. Derek Jarman also released his final film, the totally unique *Blue*: 79 minutes of a quivering blue screen and a multilayered soundtrack in which

Jarman meditates on colour, sight, sex, religion and death. Jarman died from HIV in early 1994.

In Australia 1994 was the year when there was a sudden flurry of mainstream gay-themed films with the release of *Priscilla Queen of the Desert* and *The Sum of Us*. In New Zealand Peter Jackson gave us *Heavenly Creatures*. In the US we saw Rose Troche's *Go Fish* the first of the lesbian 'Indies'. Alan Hollinghurst's novel *Folding Star* was shortlisted for the Booker prize and the *Penguin Book of Gay Short Stories* attempted a historical survey of gay writing. And emerging queer literature was large enough to include a mainstream writer like Hollinghurst as well as mavericks like Robert Gluck who in the same year published one of my all-time favourites, his fantasia on 14th century English mystic Margery Kempe where he overlays a retelling of Margery's story with his own experience of an impossible love affair.

It was also the time when the movement for civil partnerships and same-sex marriage was building momentum. Norway had formalised registered partnerships in 1993 and the Supreme Court of Hawaii ruled in Baehr v. Lewin that a same-sex marriage ban was unconstitutional unless the state could present a 'compelling state interest' to prove otherwise. This began the raft of Defence of Marriage acts in US state and federal legislatures that would mark US LGBTI politics for over a decade. In 1994 Sweden joined Norway in recognising registered partnerships. But it would be another six years before the Netherlands would become the first state in the world to recognise same-sex marriage.

So here again we see that arc towards liberation but the fragility of the moment.

The early 90s also saw the emergence of what is now called queer theory which was an attempt to go beyond assimilationist models of 'gay' or 'lesbian' to a radical celebration of difference. And Judith Butler introduced us to the idea of gender as performance, sexuality as performance, a performance that is highly ritualised and regulated but one that can at any point be destabilised, questioned, reperformed.

Fear of a Queer Planet[1], a seminal collection of academic essays published in 1993, sought to synthesise some of these new threads

in emerging queer theory. Michael Warner writes in his
introduction to that volume:

> What do queers want? This volume takes for granted that
> the answer is not just sex ... queer politics may have
> implications for any area of social life. Following Marx's
> definition of critical theory as 'the self-clarification of the
> struggles and wishes of the age', we might think of queer
> theory as the project of elaborating, in ways that cannot be
> predicted in advance, this question: What do queers want?
>   For most part, left traditions of social and political
> theory have been unwilling to ask the question. They have
> posited and naturalised a heterosexual society. For left social
> theorists this book suggests how queer experience and
> politics might be taken as starting points rather than as
> footnotes. At the same time, this book urges lesbian and
> gay intellectuals to find new engagement with various
> traditions of social theory. (vii)

We could almost take this as an introduction to *The Erotic
Contemplative* if we replaced 'left traditions' with 'church' and
'social theorists' with 'theologians':

> *For most part, the church and mystical tradition have been
> unwilling to ask the question. They have posited and naturalised
> a heterosexual church. For theologians this book suggests how
> queer experience and politics might be taken as starting points
> rather than as footnotes. At the same time, this book urges
> lesbian and gay intellectuals to find new engagement with
> various traditions of theology.*

So, while I think that *The Erotic Contemplative* is in one sense
quite a unique work that is still in many ways unmatched in what it
does, I also want to place it in its time where many people from
many different traditions were trying to *restory queer sexuality* –
placing queer experience alongside other traditions, adding to,
enlivening and challenging those traditions.
   Rethinking what it means to be married.

Rethinking what it means to be gendered.

Rethinking what it means to live or to die with HIV.

Performing lesbian, gay, queer in a new way.

The first part of Kushner's *Angels in America* ends with the Angel crashing through the roof and proclaiming, 'The Great Work has begun', and at the end of part two Prior assures us that The Great Work needs to continue and that it will continue.

And I think there was a real sense at this time that something was changing, that there was Great Work that needed to be done, and that we had to be part of that change. It's what Christians call building the kingdom, and kingdom politics are complex: it's what gave us Martin Luther King; but it's also what gave us Jerry Falwell.

Michael talks about this sense of the here-but-not-here great kingdom in his lecture on liberation. He recalls sitting in Berkeley with some friends from Nicaragua who had been deeply involved in the liberation struggle in that country …

> I said to my friend Elena, 'You know, it's not going to happen. It's really not going to happen. We've been struggling for the kingdom of justice and peace for 2000 years, in one community after another after another. And now we're struggling in Nicaragua. And we're struggling in the United States, and we're struggling in Tasmania, and we're struggling in all these countries around the world for gay liberation. In some true sense, it's not going to happen. And if it happens in this community, it'll be fragile, and it may well fall apart. And if it doesn't, there will be other communities where we still have to struggle. Our whole lives go into this. In Nicaragua, they say, maybe our struggle will bear fruit in 200 years' time, in our great grandchildren's time. We hope it does, we can only give our lives for the struggle'. So I said to her, 'in a sense it's not going to happen. And in another sense, it's already happened. Because look at people like you (this beautiful incredible woman sitting across from me), look at people like Raphael who's a leader in the older peace community in

Nicaragua, look at women like Ersacillia from way out in the sticks in the desert parts of Nicaragua who lives and struggles and reflects and prays and works with her community. These are the people in whom already the kingdom is alive. (142)

I think this is the central challenge that Michael gives us in these lectures. He is asking: where is this fight for justice alive in us? He asks us to address our 'moment of truth', and tells us that our actual historical lives and our spiritual lives, our outer and inner lives are not sperate as these expressions may indicate.

Michael meditates on key themes of liberation, exile, uncertainty, darkness, the instinct toward the unnameable mystery, the instinct towards community and shared belief, the necessity of resistance, the struggle for justice, the need for openness and receptivity, the fire that all this causes in our bodies, the will to love, desire, and to be consumed in the eyes of the other.

And in all this he speaks as a gay man, he speaks as a Christian, and he speaks as a human being vividly alive in the crazy world of 1994 that was calling out for new stories, new ways of being, new modes of performance.

He invokes key figures, Moses and exodus, Jesus and liberation, John of the Cross and the dark night. Finally, in his concluding lecture, he takes us through a beautiful and expansive meditation on what has always been one of my favourite Gospel stories, where two disciples meet Jesus on the day of the resurrection as they head out of town toward a city called Emmaus, he comes along and walks with them but they don't recognise him (Luke 24:13-35).

As these two men walk along, Luke tells us, they were talking together about 'all that had happened' and then as Jesus appears, and starts to walk besides them, he joins in their talk and, Luke says, he starts to open their eyes … You're talking about these things, but you don't understand them … If you want to understand these events you have to look at their meaning in the context of history … And Jesus starts to talk them through the tradition, but not as a set of ancient stories, as living history inflected with *all that had just happened*.

So, in the end, I think the challenge of *The Erotic Contemplative* is not to just to remember the events of 1994 but to look at 'all that has happened' right now ... The pandemic, Black Lives Matter, the continuing struggle of queer people in many parts of the world, particularly the struggle of trans people to be recognised for who they are .... What is happening now and how can we understand this as emerging from a past and travelling into a future? How can we feel this in our bodies and commit to do something about it?

I'll end with a quote from Michael:

> The spiritual life is not a cocoon where we can just be safe from any danger. Quite the opposite. The spiritual life is the risk of all that we are, of our whole life itself. And very often in living the spiritual life, we feel that our very life is on the line. And it truly is. It's also a place of hope, a hope that is, in some ways, unable to be grasped or even expressed. But it's hope that keeps us alive, keeps us going through the night. (138)

In *The Erotic Contemplative* Michael points to the hard work of kingdom politics and marshals a wonderful *restorying of the queer spiritual journey* that almost twenty years later still continues to offer us hope.

---

1. *Fear of a Queer Planet: Queer Politics and Social Theory*, ed. Michael Warner (University of Minnesota Press, 1993)

Something I had to Do

Nanette McGregor

Nan McGregor passed away in April 2022 as this book was being prepared for publication. AB

I was very involved in my local church.[1] I used to write liturgy, and my whole family would go to mass. This was when the children were young.

We always supported our son Kieran, sensing early on that he was gay, and made our house open to any of our kids' friends. But Kieran wasn't always supported by the church. At his Catholic boys' school, he was on his own. The sports master gave him hell. One day, Kieran asked to see the principal, who said to him, 'Technically, Kieran, you are a sinner.' Because Kieran was gay.

And the church didn't always support me or the rest of my family either. Our church ostracised us because I came out in support of Kieran. But I had to. When people are doing wrong, you have to speak up for the good ones. I had to speak up for my son and all the people the church was hurting.

Meeting Michael

I was looking for the support that I wasn't getting from the church, and I found what I was looking for from my religion in Michael Kelly. I first met Michael when St. John Vianney's in Springvale

---

[1] At the time of this interview, Nan was in her mid-80s, frail of body but still feisty of spirit and as sharp as ever about justice and inclusion. We are honoured to have the words and reflections of this remarkable woman within this collection.

In the interview conducted by Dr Maria Pallotta-Chiarolli and edited by Andrew Brown, Nan explains that while she and her husband John were engaged in the movement for change in the broader community through PFLAG, they, along with their son Kieran, faced many challenges within their local church communities. Enter Michael, who, in co-founding the Rainbow Sash Movement, enabled Nan and many others to articulate and challenge the Catholic Church's discriminatory teaching on homosexuality.

advertised him as a guest speaker. I wanted to listen to him because I used to go to a parents' group at the school across the road. I thought he'd be an interesting person to have come and speak to us, but he was more than that. He was charismatic. He was speaking about the church's attitude to gay people, and I thought, 'What a man!' He was a powerful speaker. And I thought, 'I've got to get to know him personally, beyond just listening to him talking about the role of church and school in relation to gay people, especially gay young people.'

Around the kitchen table

Michael used to come to our home and have dinner with us. More and more, we had lots of group meetings about how to improve the church and how to keep action bowling along. We would plan together around the kitchen table, and then we would break up from the meeting, and Michael and I would just talk. Over time, Michael became a dear friend to us.

Wearing the Rainbow Sash

In the early days, as we were getting to know Michael, he was laying the foundations for the Rainbow Sash Movement. And I thought, 'What a wonderful idea! They've got to know with the Rainbow Sash that we are Catholics, and we want to be accepted into the Church.' George Pell, the Archbishop of Melbourne at the time, was putting up this barrier. I remember when he said to the media, 'Being gay is a bigger health hazard than smoking.'

When we went to the Cathedral for mass wearing the rainbow sash, I purposely chose to stand before George Pell for communion. He looked down at me and said, 'Take that bit of rag off.'

I replied, 'I can't. It's a rainbow. And the rainbow is a symbol in the sky.'

He said, 'I'll give you a blessing.'

I held up my finger to him and said, 'No, I don't want a blessing. I want to receive communion.' The approach of The Rainbow Sash Movement was not to engage in conversation with those giving out communion, but I was determined I was going to let Archbishop Pell know how I felt. I said, 'One day, God is going to have to forgive you or find a way to bless <u>you</u>.'

I was up the front of the communion line. When I looked up at him with my finger raised, everything seemed to go quiet. I was hoping I could get through to him as a mother. I said, 'I'm a heterosexual mother. I happen to love my gay son.' All he could do was wag his head at me.

After mass, out the front of the cathedral, George Pell mingled with the congregation and those that supported his behaviour. But not all in the congregation supported him. Some were shocked at what had happened. One woman said, 'Wearing the sash shouldn't stop you from receiving communion.' Another said, 'Good on you, you're doing the right thing.'

Michael was there too of course, and some of the journalists said, 'One thing we love about Michael is that he gives us the best lines to put out there.' They were totally with us. There were photos in *The Australian* and *The Age* the next day. Of the whole lot of us.

We went back to the Cathedral many times. At the designated time during the mass, we would stand up wearing our rainbow sashes. Some people in the pews would frown and look all upset, but then others would begin to stand up too.

I just felt I had to be part of Michael's Rainbow Sash. I was determined to confront George Pell and others like him in the church.

Michael's legacy

Michael was a wonderful man, and he had a wonderful approach to people. He was really charismatic and a brilliant speaker, with a way of communicating that nobody else had.

Michael fostered a community of love around the Rainbow Sash and in all that he did. There was a photograph on the front page of *The Age* after one of our actions at the cathedral. I remember being very upset. I had burst into tears because of the rejection we had all experienced. One of the Rainbow Sash gay men and a young lesbian woman have their arms around me. We all supported each other, and all worked side-by-side with Michael in trying to make change.

The church, and even some other Catholic gay people, saw him as a troublemaker, a rabble rouser. But he was a peacemaker. He was only questioning and challenging. He said what needed to be said. His legacy will live on through the many people's lives he touched.

Doing what's right is the best way to honour Michael's legacy.

Pray, Believe, Live: The Queer Mystical Liturgical Life of Michael Bernard Kelly

John Xavier Rolley

'Why does he torture himself with the perceived cruelty of his Church in its dealing with him?'… He cannot let go because of love.[1]

The Honourable Justice Michael Kirby AC CMG

In offering this contribution, I seek to do something that, in all honesty, is quite impossible: to present, albeit fleetingly, a picture of Michael Bernard Kelly's liturgical imagination with its many wells, and its prayerful life-full expression. It is written to give thanks for and to honour Michael. Yet, more importantly, to challenge others to catch some of his flame and transform it in their living, praying and loving. It is not written as a monument of virtual marble and gold, but in flesh and heart, spirit and mind.

The liturgy of the Christian church is its heart and soul and incorporates the breadth of expression of the People of God in its birthing, loving, living and dying. The Eucharist stands as the pinnacle of that living and expresses the core of human desire for connection with God and the response of God's desire for connection with God's people. Yet, it is critical to note that the heart and soul of liturgy itself is the very people for whom the liturgy exists. It is from the people that the words, the ritual, the movement and symbols flow to the One who creates, redeems and sanctifies; God, the source of all being. The people, gathered in faith, and out of the fullness of human living, is the principal way in which Christ is made present.[2] That presence bears witness to the height of human beauty, as reflected in the face of Christ our Beloved, while standing in the realities of the entangled, broken, hopeful, joyful, grief-ful nature of incarnate living. Yet, Christ is present, ever present, longingly present and lovingly present.

Liturgy is the heart of Christian life. It expresses belief, conveys longing and empowers the people for service. Like much of Christianity's nomenclature, the term derives from Greek meaning 'the work of the

---

[1] Kelly MB, *Seduced by Grace: Contemporary spirituality, Gay experience and Christian faith* (Melbourne: Clouds of Magellan Press, 2007). The quote is from the Foreword graciously written by the Honourable Michael Kirby AC CMG
[2] Sacrasanctum Concillium [Constitution on the Liturgy], The Second Vatican Council.

people'.[3] The focus on 'the people', in particular the marginalised, disenfranchised and dispossessed of the People of God, formed a driving locus of Michael Bernard Kelly's liturgical imagination. That imagination was characterised by a deep grounding in the Church's theological, liturgical and mystical traditions, formed by emerging cosmological realisations of the place of humanity and our world within the universe, and underscored with the imperative of justice proclaimed in the Gospels. Justice drove Michael to stand up, speak up, act up and pray up for those repressed by our world's powerful and broken structures; the Church being a pertinent example. His move to ordination as a deacon, priest and bishop, outside of the Roman Church of his birth and nurture, underscores his vocational urge to spread a table of justice around which the alienated could experience the love of Christ drawing them in gathering around Word and Sacrament.

Michael's living, particularly grounded in the earthiness of his humanity and masculinity, became a conduit of grace. A grace characterised by a mystical and liturgical way of being that helped build communities of God's love: His presence also reflected truth to the powerful that often elicited painful responses and further alienation. Yet even those moments were graced liturgically.

Michael's liturgical legacy isn't a legacy in terms of being monumental, fixed and immovable. Rather, his legacy is enfleshed in the hearts and minds of those with whom and for whom he laboured. His liturgical imagination is less a sacramentary[4] and more a way of being and living in the face of injustice. As such, the deep consistency of Michael's theology was expressed in his personal and corporate prayer life and made evident in how he lived: *Lex orandi, lex credeni, lex vivendi*[5]. Amen.

The Incarnation: God in Human Flesh

Michael's liturgical theology was grounded in the Incarnation: an enfleshed reality of the Emmanuel presence. The incarnation takes place in the midst of the realities of human birthing, growing, loving, living and dying; in the

---

[3] Λιτιγιουσ may mean either 'work of the people' or work 'for the people'. Whatever the interpretation, the emphasis is on the notion that the prayer life of the People of God is firmly the business of the priesthood of all the baptised.
[4] A sacramentary is an 'official' collection of liturgical works, mostly Eucharistic, used by a church as their standard and authorised forms of worship.
[5] Simply put: Consistency between how one prays, what one believes and how one lives.

midst of our beauty and grotesque; compassion and violence. Christ came not as a rarefied pure yet corporeal ghostly apparition, rather a fully in-fleshed human endowed with opportunity for light and shadow. Equally, Christ did not come simply as the peasant itinerant preacher, Jesus, with some good old-fashioned home-spun wisdom that someone jotted down and passed on.[6] It is no accident that the Christ of the incarnation was born of a very young woman, barely old enough to marry, from the rural backwater of Palestine; poor, vulnerable and marginalised. For Michael, the marginal realities of the incarnation sat at the nexus between Jesus the Christ, The Word becoming flesh at the margins, and the fullness of his human reality. Michael prayed into this mystery from a Eucharistic Preface he wrote:

> In the fullness of time,
> your spirit hovered over the womb of a young woman, Mary, who
> opened herself to you with trust.
> In her body and through her '*fiat*',[7]
> your love became fully human,
> became a vulnerable, beautiful baby.
> This child come to share with us grace upon Grace[8],
> would grow up to give heart and voice
> and embodiment to your divine mystery,
> and would, in dying,
> open his arms to the whole of creation
> and pour forth your spirit as a living gift.[9]

---

[6] National Conference of Catholic Bishops, *The Sacramentary* (New York: Catholic Book Publishing Company, 1985). The nature of Christ was a significant theological issue for MBK. Michael held to a Christology grounded in the Creeds: I believe in one Lord, Jesus Christ, the only Son of God, eternally begotten of the Father, God from God, Light from Light, true God from true God, begotten not made, one in being with the Father. Through him all things were made. For us [men] and for our salvation he came down from heaven...

[7] *fiat* is Michael's personal motto. That self-giving and total abandonment to the will of God.

[8] John 1:16

[9] John Xavier Rolley, Irene Wilson, and Michael Bernard Kelly, An Order of Holy Eucharist, 2015, The Emmaus Community, Melbourne. The Preface. Michael wrote and edited this Preface over many years. First using a version with various groups within Australia and the United States, it became a part of the Emmaus' community's liturgy particularly on major celebrations such as Christmas and Easter. A form of it was used as part of his Funeral celebrations.

The incarnation forms the bedrock of Michael's liturgical and eucharistic imagination. It was part of the embrace of the cataphatic[10] way of standing in awe and wonder of the deeply cosmological miracle of the Incarnation.[11]

Nowhere is this Incarnational imagination expressed more fully for Michael than in the Eucharist. As a deeply formed Catholic[12], the Eucharist was the height of communal celebration deeply rooted in the belief that all are called from Baptism to minister. The Eucharist wasn't reserved for the holy and pure, rather broken open for all who seek God's love. The Eucharist was for the building up of the people to be a blessing to all.

Re-membered Eros: Entering the Full Incarnation of Human Flesh in God

The Christian Church has a long history of distrust of the human body with its inherent connection to sexual expression leading often to extreme repression and demonisation. Yet, examples of profound mystical experiences of God painted with the colours and hues of human eroticism break through to create transformative visions of re-membered, healed, embodied loving. Two such examples that influenced Michael's spirituality were Sts Teresa of Avila and John of the Cross. The latter, in particular, whose poem, which opens the treatise on the soul's relationship with God, The Dark Night of the Soul, served as a personal anthem[13] as well as a point of reflection in several liturgical contexts. One in particular was the final Eucharist of an Advent retreat conducted at Easton Mountain, New York.

---

[10] There are two primary approaches to mystical theology in the Christian tradition: Apophatic – the 'via negativa', which attempts to describe God by what God is not. In terms of mystical practice, it is often associated with 'detachment' or κενοσιζ (kenosis) meaning 'emptying'. Cataphatic – the 'via positiva', which seeks to experience God through the created order. Love mysticism is an example of the cataphatic approach, and is discussed further in this essay.

[11] Kelly MB, *Christian Mysticism's Queer Flame: Spirituality in the Lives of Contemporary Gay Men* (New York: Routledge, 2018), 33-34.

[12] As many will be aware, Michael was excommunicated from the Roman Catholic Church. From the margins of exile, he was drawn into the Old Catholic movement and lived out his incarnational baptismal ministry through the Diaconate, Priesthood and Episcopate. Catholic, in this sense, means both the in-fathomable roots of the Catholic tradition, as well as the breadth of the contemporary church. His catholicity meant there were no margins, just the presence of Christ with us, in all its forms, dark and light.

[13] The Loreena McKennitt version of 'The Dark Night of the Soul' featured as one of the last pieces of music played at Michael's funeral.

A version of the poem set to music by Loreena McKennitt was the theme of this Eucharist. In that sacred space, an interpretation of the San Damiano Icon[14] had been written with the Christ as he would have been crucified, naked. The stark and confronting reality of the full masculine humanity of the Beloved struck deeply in those present. Jesus, the Man, was Jesus a man. While the hetero-normative interpretation of the Dark Night poem terms the soul as 'she', for Michael, a Queer man longing for deep union with the Beloved, the soul is male. The tryst between the soul and the Beloved is at once spiritual and erotic. The joining together, itself deeply sacramental, with the interior transformation due to an encounter of the One who gives Himself wholly and without reserve. The succumbing of the soul to the touch of the Beloved, dissolves delusions and the soul falls into the depths of the Beloved's embrace, releasing all to Him, '… abandoning my cares, among the lilies forgotten'.[15] For Michael, this is[16] not mere abstraction. It is his fulfilled realisation in God's love, and it was the foundation of his liturgical and sacramental imagination.

Michael is known internationally for his contemplative and academic explorations of the erotic within human life, Christian mysticism, and the wider church. In particular, the reclamation of the blessedness of human sexuality. While Michael's educational and academic work focused on the connection between the erotic and the experience of queer people, particularly gay men, his liturgical expression of human erotic life was broader. In particular, the acknowledgement of the feminine as an integrally infused enfleshed reality of human, and specifically, Christian life aimed at challenging the Church to rethink how it languages prayer and thereby how it honours and cares with[17] women.

---

[14] The San Damiano Icon is a replica of the cross before which St Francis of Assisi was praying when he is said to have received the commission from God to rebuild the Church. This icon is sacred to Franciscans as a symbol of their mission.

[15] Starr M, *Saint John of the Cross: Devotions, Prayers & Living Wisdom* (Louisville, CO: Sounds True, 2008). 25.

[16] I use the term 'is' rather than 'was' as he is now living into the fullness of his deeply embodied theology.

[17] Within my academic nursing experience, the notion of 'caring for' only perpetuates powerlessness with the one being 'cared for' dependent on the 'carer' for power. Caring 'with' engages partnership at the heart of the relationship. Jesus came alongside, got down in the dust with, lived and grieved with humanity. The Gospel calls us to do no less than serve 'with'.

The 'Blood and Sex' Mass[18]

One of the most poignant liturgical expressions of Eucharist was developed for the Presentation of Christ in the Temple, or, as it was known in Pre-Vatican II liturgies (both Roman Catholic and Anglican rites) as the Purification of the Blessed Virgin Mary.[19] The liturgy combines symbols of water (preferably sea water)[20] and fire to represent the feminine and masculine aspects of human living. Both are imbued with the mystical, as such, the spiritual and erotic. The last time that rite was celebrated was with a group called Inclusive Catholics who were longing to see the realisation of women being ordained as priests within the Roman Catholic Church.

The service was a synergy of two sections, Word and Sacrament, celebrated in a unique way. Once the two symbols of water and fire were placed, a series of prayers accompanied by movement proceeded to each of the four cardinal points. In each place, women prayed for the Church that it would turn from its sins against women. Water was sprinkled, prayers said. The Word broken open, time for prayer and reflection. The following excerpts are provided to give liturgical textual context to this discussion and include: A prayer over the water; Prayer at the Eastern Wall; and Final Blessing.[21] In each, you will see the threads of Michael's liturgical vision and how they connect in the prayer of the Church.

Prayer over the Water[22]

Loving and ever-creating God
We bless you for this, your holy gift of water.
We give thanks for earth's vast, life-giving oceans,
for her hidden aquifers and tranquil lakes,

---

[18] The subtitle comes from a person who attended the Eucharistic celebration described in this section. They were offended by the ways in which Michael, Irene Wilson and myself had incorporated the enfleshed human experiences of women, and by deep connection, all of humanity, within the prayers, movement and celebration of the Eucharist.

[19] Kelly MB, *Seduced by Grace* (Melbourne: Clouds of Magellan Press, 2007), 238.

[20] Sea water invokes both the primordial sea from which life emerged, tears shed and the amniotic fluid of birth.

[21] All excerpts were written by Michael with the exception of the Eucharistic Preface, which was written by me and edited with Michael.

[22] Written by Michael Kelly, the first of a series of prayers used in the liturgy. Following this blessing prayer, a prayer in the east, north, west, south and centre were given followed by a final blessing.

for the rains, the rivers, the sacred springs.
We bless you for the water of our own bodies,
For our sweat, our tears, our spit,
For the flow of our blood and the fluids of our loving,
For the waters of the womb.
Stir again, O God, within this clear water.
May it cleanse and renew, soften and sweeten, purify and bring new life.
Through the Water and the Holy Spirit, may we be born again as your Church
And live always as your people.
We ask this in joy and hope,
Amen.

Prayer Facing the Centre

Come Spirit of the Centre, Spirit of the hidden places of our hearts!
Come, stir within us!
Rise with power and passion and holy joy!
Sweep away the last traces of shame from our lives, and open us to the wonder of our own incarnation.
Seduce us into your endless dance of erotic joy, and teach us to live with hearts held open to all that is human and everything that is earthy.
Send us forth to bring your freedom to all who live in darkness and the shadow of death.
Send us forth in the power of your Spirit and our church shall be re-created, and you will renew the face of the earth.
Come Sophia Spirit, Rise in the midst of your people!

Final Blessing

God of Life, God of Love,
Giver of all joy, teach us to live with integrity and passion.
Teach us to love with tenderness and freedom.
Let us become prophets of hope,
Servants of justice that your people come to know life in all its
abundance and open their souls to the mystery and diversity of your
endlessly creative heart.
We ask this through Jesus, our brother, our lover and our Lord.
Amen.

The altar was bare. At the offertory, women from every generation present
brought out six metres of blood red silk and draped it over the altar and
down onto the floor. Two more women brought the candles for the altar.
Others brought bread, wine and water. The Eucharistic prayer, written for
the service, was prayed by a priest while two women handled the elements,
each dressed in a white alb. The women elevated the Body and Blood of the
Beloved and distributed them to the Body. I was the priest rostered for the
day. It was a deeply humbling and grief-filled moment as a priest, who
happened to be a woman, should have presided. It represents one of the
most profound liturgical moments of my life. I know Michael and Irene felt
the same. The Eucharistic Preface I wrote and edited with Michael is
presented below:

> God our Loving Mother, with joy and thankfulness we play and
> dance around you, inhaling the warmth of your loving presence, and
> basking in the compassion of your gaze.
>
> From before the first urge of time, you embraced the seas of universal
> potential as a mother embraces, in her flesh, the ocean of her
> pregnant womb.
>
> Wherever your touch was felt, life exploded in love. You consecrated
> all life in its myriad diversity. You gave life its undying tenacity so it
> would yearn always to remain connected in you.
>
> Yet humanity drew back in fear from your feminine gifting and
> exchanged the veil of sacred mystery for a shroud of dark distrust,
> selling your daughters into the slavery of fear and disgust. And so,

your sons were blinded and lost their connection with you, their Mother's heart.

From the womb of your compassion, you called to your children, a call made warm in flesh through the womb of your daughter, Mary. And so Jesus, born through the pain, blood and anguish of a mother's love, came among us all to cast aside the shroud of distrust and to set the captives free; to proclaim the eternal healing joy of your feminine heart, O God.

In spite of all this, your church has often sought to reweave the dark shroud and reforge the chains to enslave our sisters, your daughters. Yet in Christ's love, they are ever vanquished and freedom is proclaimed to all.

And so, let us all rejoice with angels and archangels, with women and men, saints and sages from age to age, and the whole company of earth and heaven, as we sing with one voice, the unending song of praise!

A Devotion to Christ Who Carries the Wounds of the World

Michael had a particular devotion to the Five Wounds of Christ. While not the most in-vogue devotion, for Michael, it represented the ways in which Christ was present on that dark Good Friday in Jerusalem, and more importantly, how Christ continues to carry those wounds for all. The marginal place of death, the derision and rejection, all seeping into the earth as an eternal witness of God's love. As such, Good Friday, for Michael, formed a particularly sacred moment within the depths of the Holy Three Days that formed the emotional rollercoaster ride of Holy Week and Easter. Without this soul wrenching day, there is no Resurrection, no Ascension.

Jesus' coming into the social, political and economic realities of Israel's story was critical for Michael's ministry as a forth-teller of the Gospel. The themes of justice for the orphaned, widowed, outcast, alien, leper and even eunuch[23], emerge from the deep streams of the ancient Jewish prophets. It is from this same stream, that Michael's liturgical being was nourished.

---

[23] Tonstad LM, *Queer Theology*, Cascade Companions, (Eugene, OR: Cascade Books, 2018). Note: The 'eunuch' is an important theme in Queer theology and represents that 'outsider' who sits on the edges of the People of God, yet is

Upon speaking with Michael shortly after his diagnosis with bowel cancer, I wrote a Novena (Please see the Appendix for a copy of the Novena)[24] for him based on his devotion to the Five-Wounds of Christ. It embodied, for me, the life he shared in his Beloved Christ. Michael's life was characterised by significant physical suffering and so found a profound connection with the sufferings of the Beloved. As a result, he had an immense empathy for suffering in others and saw the Beloved in their contexts of suffering.

Embodied Resurrection – The Road from Emmaus

Nowhere does Michael's liturgical imagination emerge more fully than in his explication of the scriptural account of the Road to Emmaus.[25] In that account, two disciples journey away from Jerusalem following the horrific events of the Passover. They are part of the stream of humanity that the Word, the Sacraments, and the empowering presence of the Beloved will come together to transform.

Michael had a thoroughly Catholic Sacramental Theology which served as the weft and foundation of his fabric, through which the threads of justice, the cries of the marginalised, the realities of a broken Church and the profoundly confronting Presence of Christ wove its pattern. For many, it was ugly and deformed. No-one wants to hear about the realities of human living, loving and dying in their prayers. Yet, it is in the midst of the grief of rejection, oppression and the unrelenting call of the Spirit to bear witness to the margins of our world that drove Michael. And, yes, at times it was ugly.

The most empowering element of the story is that despite the marginalised and demoralised nature of the two disciples leaving Jerusalem, Jesus came to the margins of their experience, breaking open the Word and opening their eyes in the breaking of bread. The depth of meaning doesn't

---

covered by God's command to the people to honour and shelter them as if they were an essential part of the congregation.

[24] A Novena is a prayer said for nine consecutive days. It usually involves a specific intention and devotion to either a Saint of the Church or other devotion (for example, the Sacred Heart, the Holy Spirit, the Blessed Virgin).

[25] For deeper insight into Michael's understanding of the Road to Emmaus, please see his essay 'The Road from Emmaus: the challenge of the future' in Kelly MB, *Seduced by Grace: Contemporary Spirituality, Gay Experience, and Christian Faith* (Melbourne: Clouds of Magellan Press, 2007), 26. It is a deeply moving exegesis of the passage.

linger there, however. Tellingly, following this encounter, the disciples take to the road once more, but this time, they journey from Emmaus back to Jerusalem. It is from the margins that Jesus compels us to be witness bearers, justice keepers, diversity embracers and lovers! The marginalised carry equally the vocation to be Christ the Beloved to our broken world – to pray, believe and live out of our relationship with the Beloved who draws all creation together in love.

Conclusion

Michael's liturgical imagination arose out of the deep wells of his faith and living. He prayed as he believed and lived as he prayed. I, personally, have benefited from sitting at his feet and learning the precious craft of liturgy. I will be forever grateful to God for the gift of Michael: as a man, a priest, a liturgist, a bishop and above all, a friend. This is how Blessed Michael of Melbourne lived.

Blessed Michael, pray for us!

Novena to the Five Wounds of Christ the Beloved, dedicated to Michael Bernard Kelly

Gathering

Inclusive Sign of the Cross [26]
In the Name of the Loving Creator, Compassionate Jesus and the Healing Sophia Spirit. **Amen.**

Sentence
But he was wounded for our transgressions, crushed for our iniquities; upon him was the punishment that made us whole, and by his bruises we are healed. (Isaiah 53.5)

Silence is kept.

---

[26] Inclusive Sign of the Cross: Both hands touch the forehead (In the name of the Loving Creator), both hands touch the abdomen (and of the Compassionate Christ), hands then cross to touch opposite shoulders (and of the Healing Spirit), before uncrossing to touch the opposite shoulder.

Opening Prayer

Loving God,
In whom is heaven,
I give thanks for the gift of our Beloved, Jesus, to the world.
His life of compassion brought healing and freedom to the oppressed, peace
to those who suffer in mind and body, and liberation to the poor.
I kneel before his cross and embrace his wounds, portals which drew into
himself, the suffering and death of this world.
I adore his precious wounded feet that promise liberty from oppression,
I adore his precious wounded hands which promise embrace for those who
suffer,
I adore his precious wounded side, which promises union of heaven and
earth in death's defeat.
I offer these prayers for **Michael**.
May he know the healing and liberating touch of your wounds of love.
Through Jesus Christ, our Beloved, **Amen.**

Meditation on the First Wound
Beloved Jesus, my Brother and Lover
I adore your most precious wound of your right hand which, through life,
Reached out and touched others in healing and blessing.
May your strength, in your masculine humanity, touch **Michael,** strengthen
his flesh in the face of the ravages of illness, and restore to him his power.
Defend him against the onslaught of oppression and fear as you draw him to
your heart in embrace.
Our Father …
Hail Mary, Full of Grace …
Glory be to our Loving Creator, and to our Compassionate Jesus, and to our
Healing Sophia Spirit,
As it was in the beginning, is now and forever shall be, world without end.

Meditation on the Second Wound

Beloved Jesus, my Brother and Lover
I adore your most precious wound of your left hand which, through life,
Reached out and drew all to yourself.

May your nurturing, in your feminine humanity, touch **Michael,** caress his spirit in the face of the ravages of distress and doubt, and restore to him peace.

Nourish him and renew his faith as you draw him to your heart in embrace.

Our Father ...

Hail Mary, Full of Grace ...

Glory be to our Loving Creator ...

Meditation on the Third Wound

Beloved Jesus, my Brother and Lover

I adore your most precious wound of your right foot which, through life,

Forged paths of justice in the dry and abandoned places of the world.

May your will, aligned with God's heart, embolden **Michael,** strengthen his mind in the face of the ravages of powerlessness, and restore his resolve.

Defend him against the onslaught of hopelessness as you guide him on this journey.

Our Father ...

Hail Mary, Full of Grace ...

Glory be to our Loving Creator ...

Meditation on the Fourth Wound

Beloved Jesus, my Brother and Lover

I adore your most precious wound of your left foot which, through life,

Walked with the outcast, poor and marginalised of the world.

May your faithfulness, aligned with God's passion, touch **Michael,** straighten the paths before him in the face of seemingly insurmountable obstacles, and restore to him his vision.

Defend him against the onslaught of futility as you guide him on this journey.

Our Father ...

Hail Mary, Full of Grace ...

Glory be to our Loving Creator ...

Meditation on the Fifth Wound

Beloved Jesus, my Brother and Lover

I adore your most precious wounded side,

From which blood and water flowed.

You took on our flesh and led us to partake of your divinity.

Your heart poured out compassion and promise,
healing and restoration.
May your precious wounded side, flowing with love, pour over **Michael,** and
bring him into deep union with you, that all the limitations of body and
mind may dissolve, and abundant peace prevail.
Our Father …
Hail Mary, Full of Grace …
Glory be to our Loving Creator …
Silence is kept.

Concluding Prayer

Loving God, in whom is heaven,
May the grace of your most Beloved One's wounds,
Flow to **Michael**, and bring him the fullness of healing, peace, restoration
and joy,
In your most perfect abundance and will,
I ask this through Jesus Christ, my Beloved, Brother and Lover.
Amen.

Those Called to be Saints: Queer Saintly Innovation and Belonging

Marcus O'Donnell

In one of his essays in *Seduced by Grace* Michael Kelly asks the question: 'Can a gay man be a saint?'[1] This question, to which the simplest answer might be 'Of course they can,' is in some ways at the heart of all Michael's work. In its initial meaning a saint was simply a member of the New Testament community; it's a term that Paul uses for believers throughout his letters. Here saint is a moniker of both calling and belonging: 'those called to be saints,' (1 Cor 1:2) and Michael's activism and writing were about validating the calling of ordinary queer people to be fully who they are and to find a sense of belonging in a community of believers. He dedicated *Christian Mysticism's Queer Flame*, the book that came out of his PhD project, to 'the queer saints of the future' adding: 'May their names be known, may their songs be sung.'[2] In this essay I want to meander with Michael and in memory of Michael by considering this question of *sainthood* or *saintliness* from a range of queer perspectives. Rather than ask can a gay man be a saint I want to ask: what happens when we queer sanctity?

I got to know Michael when I commissioned a number of essays as editor of gay publications *OutRage* and *Sydney Star Observer*. We discovered a shared history as gay Catholics who had been drawn deeply to the monastic tradition. Michael weaved in and out of my life for twenty years as he visited Sydney and then again when, more recently, I moved back to Melbourne. There were long gaps where we had no contact, but it was always easy to begin that single long conversation again when we reconnected. This essay continues that conversation.

The conversation about saintliness takes place today in surprisingly diverse settings: in the church of course, but also in our contemporary media culture of celebrity where charism is often gilded as a marker of saintliness, and in the world of politics and activism where lives are dramatically stretched and given for others.

---

[1] Kelly MB, *Seduced by Grace: Contemporary Spirituality, Gay Experience, and Christian Faith* (Melbourne: Clouds of Magellan Press, 2021).
[2] Kelly MB, *Christian Mysticism's Queer Flame: Spirituality in the Lives of Contemporary Gay Men* (New York: Routledge, 2018).

The conversation about queer saintliness also has a long pedigree. It can be found in the legend of Roman soldier lovers Saints Sergius and Bacchus, in the letters about holy friendship of Saint Aelred of Rievaulx, and in the unmistakable homoeroticism of the continuously dying Sebastian. Jean Genet the French queer novelist, playwright and sometime petty thief said that saintliness was the most beautiful word in human language. It held the allure of perfection, the scent of ecstasy, the extreme masochistic abandon of the body. When Jean Paul Sartre came to write a study of Genet, he called it *Saint Genet*. For the thief it was both an honour and a violation to have himself dissected and explained by the great philosopher. The saint is inexplicable. The saint can't be psychoanalysed. So, although at first, he played along with Sartre, ultimately, it wasn't a book in which Genet recognised himself. This speaks to the elusive figure of the saint, who can't be held down by our theorising or theologising. The saint is never just one thing. The saint is a leaky object.

Queer theologian Marcella Althaus-Reid continues this theme of the doubling of the saint, suggesting that a true queering of saintliness involves an embrace of the demonic that allows us to claim rebelliousness as core to saintliness.[3] And this rebellion, this *possession*, is always embodied. In *Christian Mysticism's Queer Flame*, Michael suggests, following Althaus-Reid's lead: 'we need to disrupt Christian mystical texts and mystical talk with contemporary, sexually transgressive stories, with … actual erotic desires and experiences.'[4]

Saintliness is always both a political and a spiritual identity and, as he was acutely aware, Michael's question about gay saints is therefore both a political and a spiritual one. But only rarely does the true queerness of saintliness, as understood by someone like Althaus-Reid or Genet, emerge from the more mundane spiritual politics of saint making.

---

[3] Althaus-Reid M, *The Queer God* (New York: Routledge, 2004).
[4] Kelly MB, *Christian Mysticism's Queer Flame: Spirituality in the Lives of Contemporary Gay Men* (New York: Routledge, 2018), 198.

Saints and saint-making

Anthropologist June Macklin suggests that traditionally the saint emerges from a 'storytelling triad.'[5] The saint themselves, and the anecdotes of their life, is the first part of this triad. Strangely, Macklin says, they are the least important element. What takes that life, that collection of anecdotes, and makes it saintly is not the individual themselves but the community of believers who form the other two elements of the triad: the saint's devotees and then the religious authorities who validate that devotion. These authorities 'shape and tailor the final story to fit (or modify) prefigured models, approve it, and turn the saint into a mnemonic unit.'[6]

In the Catholic tradition, from the point of view of the church, canonisation is not the celebration of a life, it is the process of putting that life on trial. It is the weighing of the prospective saint's virtue and an attempt to do away with reasonable doubt. It is jurisprudence, and jurisprudence is always about the definition and enforcement of boundaries.[7]

But boundaries are often porous and the three stories of the saint: the life, the cult and the processes of canonical jurisprudence are not always in synch. We have saints who are recognised by their communities but not by the authorities just as we have saints condemned by authorities who are later rehabilitated through the persistence of communities. Joan of Arc's burning at the stake is the most recognisable example of this but many saints have

---

[5] Macklin J, *Saints and Near-Saints in Transition* in Hopgood JF (ed.), *The Making of Saints: Contesting Sacred Ground* (Tuscaloosa, AL: University of Alabama Press, 2005), 3.

[6] ibid.

[7] Jenny Ponzo in a recent article outlining changes to the canonisation process puts it this way: 'Although many religions and cultures recognize exemplary figures representing models of perfect living, what distinguishes Catholicism in this respect is the fact that the Church has formulated both an articulated normative apparatus defining what sainthood is and how it should be officially recognized, and a unique judicial procedure consisting in a post-mortem legal trial—called cause for canonization—in which the life, writings, and fame of the candidate for sainthood are scrupulously evaluated. Canonization can therefore be defined as the decision (or sentence) made by the ecclesiastic authority to grant a mandatory cult to a person whose sanctity is found to be acceptable to the authority itself. Catholic jurisprudence in matters of canonization, therefore, is based on a principle of reasonability the form of which is—quite curiously for the non-specialists—taken from the juridical judgment in penal law.' Ponzo J. The case of the 'offering of life' in the causes for canonization of Catholic Saints: The threshold of self-sacrifice. *International Journal for the Semiotics of Law-Revue internationale de Sémiotique juridique*, 33(4), 984.

been on the verge of excommunication at different points in their trajectory toward the holy.[8]

So, saintliness is always continuously coming into being; and hagiography – the narrative of saintly lives – because it is co-constructed by multiple voices is always exceeding the boundaries set for it by the church.

Edith Wyschogrod suggests in *Saints and Postmodernism* that saints no longer need have anything to do with the church.[9] She proposes that we need new ways of understanding ethics in the post-modern world where moral theory has lost its power to produce moral lives. She suggests that the *figure* of the saint allows us to move beyond theory and see a type of *embodied* ethics, of a life lived for the other, of a 'radical generosity ... a benevolence that will not be brought to a close.' She argues:

> Such saintliness is not a nostalgic return to premodern hagiography but a postmodern expression of excessive desire, a desire on behalf of the Other that seeks the cessation of another's suffering and the birth of another's joy.[10]

In focusing on this 'desire on behalf of the other' Wyschogrod makes a distinction between theists, mystics, and saints. While these three archetypes are often – certainly in the western tradition – fused together, a first step to understanding saintliness is to peel them apart. Importantly separating the theist and the mystic from the saint allows us to focus on the *acts* of the saint rather than their inner life. In outlining her framework for such a type of sanctity Wyschogrod makes several key suggestions that are useful for thinking about the queering of saints.

Firstly, the saint is a story that demands a response: 'understanding hagiography consists not in recounting its meaning but in being swept up by its imperative force. The comprehension of the saint's life ... is a practice

---

[8] Janine Peterson outlines four categories: tolerated saints who are venerated by the communities but questioned by authorities without being condemned; suspect saints are those who are investigated for heresy but for whatever reason unable to be condemned; heretical saints are those who are condemned by the authorities but who continue to be venerated after their death; and finally holy heretics who are condemned as heretical but who communities later decide are holy. Peterson JL, *Suspect saints and holy heretics: disputed sanctity and communal identity in late medieval Italy* (Ithaca, NY: Cornell University Press, 2019).
[9] Wyschogrod E, *Saints and Postmodernism: Revisioning Moral Philosophy* (Chicago, IL: The University of Chicago Press, 1990).
[10] ibid., xxiv.

through which the addressee is gathered into the narrative so as to extend and elaborate it with his/her life.'[11]

Secondly the saint has a particular relationship to time. Wyschogrod says that the 'saintly struggle on behalf of the other is a wrestling with time'. The saint has a compelling sense of 'the time that is left' because the call of the other is wide and boundless. And this urgent sense of time is one that we as listeners become embroiled in.

> The time of a saintly life as expressed in hagiographic narrative is the time-before-it-is-too-late that is, as Kierkegaard claims, lived forward but remembered backward. Each telling of the saint's story, so long as the tradition in which the narrative is embedded remains vital, is an ever-renewed soliciting of the narrative's addressees. To those situated within this tradition, hagiography hammers home its own mode of temporalization, the time-before-it-is-too-late.[12]

This vision of the saint is not a vision of what Wyschogrod calls 'common sense altruism' rather 'the saintly desire for the other is excessive and wild.'[13]

This time-before-it-is-too-late also nods to the postmodern concern with apocalypse and fragmentation. The postmodern saint mediates this apocalyptic crisis in the life of their body. This mode of crisis is native to the saint, indeed as Beth Sutherland argues saintliness entails a 'criminal ethic' (2013).[14] She reminds us that at the core of traditional sanctity is the *imitatio Christi* who died a condemned criminal and that the first saints, the martyrs, also died as opponents or criminals of the Empire. Holy disobedience is a continuous storyline throughout saintly lives from Saint Francis' refusal to obey his father's commands to conform, through to contemporaries like Jesuit Daniel Berrigan or the Catholic Worker's Dorothy Day who were each arrested and imprisoned numerous times for their peace and social justice activism.

Genet is of course the criminal saint *par excellence*. Wyschogrod shows that postmodern hagiographies like Genet's own story and the stories he writes are written under the 'sign of erasure'. All writing is a play of absence

---

[11] ibid., xxiii.
[12] ibid., 255.
[13] ibid.
[14] Sutherland B, 'Introduction' in Dickinson C (ed.), *The Postmodern Saints of France: Refiguring the Holy in Contemporary French Philosophy* (Edinburgh: A&C Black, 2013).

and presence, the explicit and the implicit, the said and the unsaid. This is particularly so in formal genres like hagiography where each story is also every other story in the genre. So, when someone like Genet comes along and reinvents or writes over the genre his erasures are also present. Wyschogrod demonstrates this with the example of Our Lady of Flowers rewriting it again with erasures:

> Genet is alone in his prison [~~monastic cell~~] where he invents the story of Divine and her circle of criminal friends [~~circle of saints~~] based on news photos of murderers [~~icons~~] ...these photos become the subject of Genet's erotic fantasies [~~contemplation~~] ...[15]

While it is always tempting to read Genet primarily as a sexual mystic, Wyschogrod reads him as an ecstatic but under her sign of the radically generous altruist. His transgression is his gift. 'Genet's characters are saints of depravity: those who desire on behalf of the other's transgressive desire.'[16]

While reading for erasure points to the underlying structure of the saintly grid and the *imitation* at the heart of saintly practice it also highlights the possibility of saintly *innovation*. Todd Mei suggests that thinking saintliness as imitation traps us in the past, but claiming saints as innovators is future focused allowing saints to become symbols of possibility.[17] Drawing on philosopher Paul Ricoeur, Mei reminds us that symbols are not signs with limited closed systems of reference. A symbol according to Ricouer always has a 'surplus of meaning'; it is an open system. If saints carry that surplus of meaning they can never really be canonised, a process which seeks to fit them into a juridical system. In queer terms even when the church seeks to tame them saints remain promiscuous.

---

[15] Wyschogrod E, *Saints and Postmodernism: Revisioning Moral Philosophy* (Chicago, IL: The University of Chicago Press, 1990), 221.
[16] ibid., 228.
[17] Mei T 'Ricoeur and the Symbolism of Sainthood: From Imitation to Innovation' in Dickinson C (ed.), *The Postmodern Saints of France: Refiguring the Holy in Contemporary French Philosophy* (Edinburgh: A&C Black, 2013).

Queering the saint

In the Christian tradition the stories of the first martyr saints became the locus for Christian differentiation, a way of sacralising what Sutherland identified as the criminal ethic of saintliness, a way of accounting for suffering as well as celebrating the courage of resistance. Interestingly Brett Krutzsch (2019) has argued that the United States LGBTQI movement is also built on the blood of martyrs and that these martyrs have been used strategically by the movement to build internal cohesion and establish external boundaries.[18] The deaths of Harvey Milk, Matthew Shepard, Tyler Clementi and Brandon Teena, to call out the most famous cases, have all played galvanising roles in highlighting homophobia and building a narrative structure for LGBTQI rights.

If we see saints as innovators, these figures are not just individual innovators, they are innovations of the community, they are innovations of storytelling. These queer martyr narratives were created at the intersection of cult, media and activism and it is at the intersection of cult, media and activism where we see their posthumous miracles performed.

A number of writers, including his own mother, have noted the dualities operating in the story of Matthew Shepard (1976-98).[19] His mother wrote that the world knows him as *Matthew* but to his family and friends he was always more simply *Matt*.[20] This diminutive immediately evokes the intimacy of the small circle, where a name is how we speak love to one another. When the martyr or the saint suddenly becomes an object of love and devotion for a much wider public, no matter how detailed and personalised the hagiography, they inevitably become an abstract witness to a cause, they become a pattern of saintliness.

The story of Matthew Shepard martyr began in October 1998 when his bashed, mangled body was left to die tied to a fence in the middle of rural Wyoming. After he was taken unconscious to a Colorado hospital, vigils suddenly erupted all over the world. He died six days later. Whatever

---

[18] Krutzsch B, *Dying to be Normal: Gay Martyrs and the Transformation of American Sexual Politics* (Oxford: Oxford University Press, 2019).
[19] cf. Middleton P, 'The Scarecrow Christ: The Murder of Matthew Shepard and the Making of an American Culture Wars Martyr' in Saloul I and van Henten JW (eds.), *Martyrdom: Canonisation, Contestation and Afterlives* (Amsterdam: Amsterdam University Press, 2020).
[20] Shepard J, 2009, *The Meaning of Matthew: My Son's Murder in Laramie, and a World Transformed* (New York: Hudson Street Press, 2009).

happened between Matt Shepard and his killers Aaron McKinney and
Russell Henderson that night, and this has been debated in the courts and in
the media, Matthew Shepard became a victim of gay hate-crime and a
martyr for queer visibility and human rights.

The killing of Matt Shepard was a horrific tragedy, a story of loss and
grief known only to his family and friends. The killing of Matthew Shepard
was a martyrdom that gathers up that loss and grief and creates a reliquary
which comes to represent the suffering and death of queer people in a
homophobic world.[21] Like the crowds in St Peter's square at the death of
Pope John Paul II chanting 'sancto subito,' (sainthood immediately) the
proclamation of Matthew Shepard as martyr began with the vigils across
America which chanted 'never again'. Matt Shepherd became Matthew
Shepard, Matthew Shepard became a movement.

Both his friends and his critics have pointed out that Matt Shepard was
no saint. He was a confused young man, somewhat depressed, struggling
with his use of drugs. If we take Wyschogrod's notion of radical generosity
as characteristic of saintliness we find examples of kindness in Matt's life but
nothing that would take this to the level of 'heroic virtue'. But in a
remarkable transformation, in death Matthew Shepard becomes in
Wyschogrod's words 'a benevolence that will not be brought to a close.' His
martyrdom created a movement which worked tirelessly to enact hate crimes
legislation, a movement that worked to codify those sanctifying chants of
'never again'. The radical generosity of Matthew Shepard comes to include
all those who act in his name.

Saints, especially queer saints are not singular bodies. Their bodies leak,
their bodies transmogrify, their bodies become one with others, their bodies
multiply, their I becomes us, becomes we, and it is we who act in their
name.

The many ways that queer saints become lives for others is complex and
certainly not only through the visceral spectacle of martyrdom.

Pauli Murray (1910-1985), lawyer, activist, poet, and priest lived a life of
firsts and as a pioneer they trailblazed pathways for others. Their innovative

---

[21] I make this statement well aware of the inherent problems with claims of
universal representation. A number of commentators have rightly pointed out that
Matthew Shepherd's whiteness and relative wealth not only prevented a range of
queer people, particularly those who are poor and Black, from seeing themselves
in him, and his canonisation as everyqueer by the media and the movement
actively occluded their lives from this definition of queer.

legal theory influenced the outcomes of key legal battles which defined the human rights of Black people and of women. These included critical contributions to the 1954 *Brown versus Board of Education* case which struck down segregation in schools, as well as being named co-author for their contribution to Ruth Bader Ginsburg's 1971 brief in *Reed versus Reed*, which struck down discrimination on the basis of sex. They were the first Black woman to get a doctorate from Yale and the first Black woman to be ordained as an Episcopal priest. In 2012 they were added to the calendar of holy men and holy women in the Episcopal church, and so along with the many other firsts Pauli might now claim to be the first officially recognised queer saint.[22]

At one level Pauli Murray's saintliness is defined by the fact that they showed no mind to race, gender or sexuality, at another level it is defined by their continuous radical struggle with these very realities. The feeling, and in Pauli's case the actuality, that no*body* had done this before. In a 'Credo' written in 1945 Murray, noting their mixed race, describes themself as 'a representative of blended humanity'. They also identify themselves in the stream of 'poets and prophets', Christ, Gandhi and Thoreau:

> I intend to do my part through the power of persuasion, by spiritual resistance, by the power of my pen, and by inviting the violence upon my own body. For what is life itself without the freedom to walk proudly before God and man and to glorify creation through the genius of self-expression? … When my brothers try to draw a circle to exclude me, I shall draw a larger circle to include them.[23]

They put their body on the line often. Murray was jailed for refusing to go to the back of the bus in 1940, fifteen years before Rosa Parks' similar action sparked a movement. Interestingly, although this pioneering moment is now

---

[22] Pauli lived and died before the pronoun wars and was called and answered to she/her. But at the heart of Pauli's saintliness there was what we might call a dark night of gender. We know from writings published after their death that Pauli lived with the deep feeling of being a man and had even explored possibilities of surgical or hormonal treatment. So, in writing them as a saint who unfolds new possibilities for others, possibilities that were not open to them, I honour their trans saintliness, I honour their plurality, with pronouns that were not possible for them in life. That I have to stop and explain myself points to the difference between the radical immediacy of the saintly life and what we might call the theologising that makes sense of the variety of claims on the saintly body.

[23] Murray P, 'An American Credo'. *Common Ground* 5(2), 1945, 22-24.

acknowledged, what is not fully acknowledged is that Murray was arrested with their lover of the time, Adelene MacBean, and Pauli was dressed as a man.[24]

Their Aunt Pauline who had raised Pauli referred to Pauli's 'boy-girl' personality and this was evident from an early age. Writing to a doctor in 1942 whom Pauli hoped would be able to provide hormone treatment, Pauli said forthrightly 'my life is somewhat unbearable in its present phase, and though a person of ability this aspect continually blocks my efforts to do the things of which I am capable'. In a later letter they added: 'What I mean is that I do an effective job over a short period of time, but my conflicts interfere with permanent long-time work and keep me constantly afraid to accept new responsibilities.'[25]

Part of Pauli's saintliness is this long, embodied struggle for both the freedom of self-expression and the freedom of others. It was a struggle where at the time there were few public words to name such an experience and so Pauli lived with this 'cloud of unknowing', which was paradoxically a wordless lonely certainty that could not be expressed. This caused much suffering but as Pauli's biographer points out it was also the source of their deepest contributions.

> In some ways, her gender-nonconforming persona made it difficult to win the recognition she might otherwise have achieved, but it also made possible her most important insight: that gender was not, any more than race, a fixed category.[26]

Long before contemporary theorists began to talk of 'intersectionality' – the contribution of multiple identities to lived experiences of embodiment and of discrimination – Pauli Murray talked of Jane Crow, the Black woman who was discriminated against on the basis of both sex and race. This idea was forged in their own *trans* gendered and *multi* racial body.

Bishop Michael Curry in celebrating Murray as a new episcopal saint said:

---

[24] Fisher SED, 'Pauli Murray's Peter Panic: Perspectives from the Margins of Gender and Race in Jim Crow America.' *Transgender Studies Quarterly*, 3(1-2), 2016, 95-103.
[25] Rosenberg R, *Jane Crow: The Life of Pauli Murray* (Oxford: Oxford University Press, 2017), 117.
[26] ibid., 2.

Pauli Murray had an agenda for the human good that was constant and unswerving. As a descendent of slaves and slaveholders … she is a symbol for the importance of bringing different worlds together, even in midst of great pain.[27]

For all their pioneering Pauli never talked or wrote publicly about their 'boy-girl' gender or their queer sexuality, but as Sarah Azaransky points out Pauli meticulously organised an archive for future scholars complete with private ponderings on gender and sexuality, a photo album of their adventures as a 'boy' traveller in the 1930s, and letters in which Pauli clearly expressed love for their female partners. In some ways Pauli remained in that 'cloud of unknowing' throughout their life; even when many others had found words to publicly claim their queerness, Pauli resisted. This was consistent with their lifelong refusal to confine themself to one place, one gender, one profession, one race, one sexuality. Queerness and saintliness for Pauli was to live in between in the space of unknowing.

When Michael asked the question that prompted this essay ('Can a gay man be a saint?') it was in an opinion piece he wrote for a Melbourne newspaper celebrating the saintliness of Fr Mychal Judge (1933-2001), the Franciscan FDNY chaplain who died on 9/11. He was also a gay priest and a well-known, well-loved maverick who was always extending himself for those in need.

Shannon Stapleton's image of Judge being carried by his five pallbearers from the Twin Towers disaster is one of the only widely circulated images of the dead bodies of 9/11. Photojournalists and media organisations are addicted to disaster but ethically averse to showing the actual dead bodies of disaster victims. Stapleton's image became an allowable image of death for a number of reasons. It is compositionally striking, it paints a picture which is at once poignant and heroic, it narrates death and disaster without exposing its macabre, bloodied tangle and the posture of Judge's body immediately locates it in a particular register of religious images of dead bodies beginning with Michelangelo's famous Pieta.

But perhaps another less obvious reason this image became an exception to the media's general rule is that it is a narrative image of the journey of the dead, rather than a static image of a victim of disaster. Because of its sense of action in stillness, movement captured but not interrupted, this photograph

---

[27] Duke Today 'Pauli Murray named to episcopal sainthood' 4 July 2012, available online: https://today.duke.edu/2012/07/saintmurray.

is an image of transition or transformation rather than one of finality: an image of becoming, which of course is the perfect spiritual metaphor for death. Christians, along with other religious traditions, believe that the moment of death is the moment of ultimate transformation: a birth, a new life, a sudden opening-up into the divine universe.

Judge and his emergency services colleagues are captured emerging from a smoke haze of dust and ash. In this process of emerging out into the light of day, emerging from the disaster, they reveal something about what lies behind the veil, what lies at the heart of disaster. It was a fitting icon for the emergent sanctity of Mychal Judge.

As Michael Kelly writes: 'In an extraordinary way his image – silent in death but potent with love – became a gift, a light that was literally beamed around the world even as the towers fell … this icon spoke not of fear or violence or despair, but of self-sacrificial love, of grace, of faith, of hope.'[28]

However, Judge did not remain merely a poignant picture of inspirational, heroic sacrifice; his myth was quickly animated, and the inert body of Shannon Stapleton's photograph became a living saint, as a *New York* magazine profile published less than two months after his death makes clear:

> Within hours of the collapse, a story began circulating that [Judge had] been hit by falling debris when he took his helmet off to give last rites to a firefighter, a man who himself had been crushed by someone who'd jumped from Tower One. Seven weeks later, it seems that the story is at least partly myth, though perhaps a myth necessary to the demands of the day. … But it's understandable how the myth bloomed. Those who knew Judge – and he knew hundreds, if not thousands, of people – wanted him to die gorgeously and aptly, in a way that expressed the depth of his faith. It was how they imagined him. Such a death suited a legend.[29]

Whatever the specifics of Judge's death, he had walked knowingly into that tower with death hanging over him. There is a video of a sermon Judge gave to fire fighters supposedly the day before 9/11. He says: 'You do what God called you to do, you show up, you put one foot in front of another, you get

---

[28] Kelly MB, *Seduced by Grace: Contemporary Spirituality, Gay Experience, and Christian Faith* (Melbourne: Clouds of Magellan Press, 2021).
[29] Senior J, 'The Firemen's Friar' (*New York*, 12 Nov. 2001).

on the rig and you go out and you do your job, which is a mystery, a surprise, you have no idea when you get on the rig, you have no idea what God's calling you to, but he needs you, he needs me, he needs all of us.'

The more that emerged about Judge's life, the clearer his popular candidature for sanctity became. Many of the vignettes are classic hagiography:

> In the early days of the AIDS epidemic, when nurses were frightened to touch people with AIDS and priests were refusing to bury them, Mychal Judge would often turn up at a hospital room unannounced. He would quietly turn back the covers on the bed of an AIDS patient and gently massage his feet. One man remembers that when his partner was dying Fr Judge came to give him Holy Communion. After the ritual the dying man anxiously whispered, 'Do you think God is angry with me?' Mychal responded by taking the man in his arms, cuddling him, rocking him against his chest, then kissing him.[30]

Although these stories are powerful and there has been a persistent popular campaign to recognise Judge's sanctity, any official process has been stymied; we can only assume this is because of his sexuality. Judge immediately presents himself as a candidate for saint under a new category of saints that Pope Francis introduced in 2007: those who give their life for others. But even when postulators close to the Vatican's Congregation for Saints have suggested that this is an obvious route, the officials of his order have failed to pursue it.[31]

As Michael Kelly wrote in a moving meditation, he delivered on Mychal Judge at New York's Union Theological Seminary:

> There is no question that Mychal repeatedly, persistently, almost obsessively put himself at the centre of situations of profound human suffering, anguish and brokenness – and into them he brought simple, deep faith, hope and love. I guess we are fine with that,

[30] Kelly MB, *Seduced by Grace: Contemporary Spirituality, Gay Experience, and Christian Faith* (Melbourne: Clouds of Magellan Press, 2021).
[31] O'Loughlin M, 'A gay saint? L.G.B.T. groups are pushing for 9/11 hero Father Mychal Judge's canonization' (*America*, 09 Sept. 2021), available online: https://www.americamagazine.org/politics-society/2021/09/09/mychal-judge-saint-9-11-241377.

impressed by that. Then we find that he, too, was suffering, anguished and broken, struggling with addictions, struggling to integrate his sexuality, struggling to accept and love himself, struggling to open himself to faith, hope and love in his own messy, complex, real, unresolved human journey – and we get unsettled.[32]

In this way Judge presents us with a deeply queered saintliness but one, Michael reminds us, that is also at the heart of any genuine saintliness: 'It is their utter honesty, their realness, their total trust in God that makes them saints, not some cold, flawless 'perfection'. They are just themselves.'[33]

Matthew Shepard, Pauli Murray and Mychal Judge show us queer lives that have become sacramental presences in the world. For varied reasons they are figures writ-large, but they are also each, figures of struggle. Shephard was a normal young man who had martyrdom thrust upon him. Murray's achievements are historic/heroic on any level, but more so as achievements carved from the precariousness and pain of their liminal identity. Judge was a recovering alcoholic and semi-closeted pastor who spent his life for others despite his inner turmoil. Their queer saintliness borrows from the hagiographic model, but it also punctures it with failure rather than smoothing it over with perfection. This punctured nomadic queer is, as Marcella Althaus-Reid suggests, 'the image of the unstable or irredeemable body of a theological subject who loves amidst insecurity and risk.'[34]

Queer failure and the dark night

Even though there are often strange detours and dark nights in saintly lives, by definition, as portraits of perfection, ultimately hagiography reinscribes failure with a heavenly glow. The insecurity and risk of the queer saint comes from a different relationship to time and a different relationship to the way.

As Wyschogrod notes, saints exist in an urgent relationship to time, they are compelled forward, but this compelling forward-motion is often tamed in traditional hagiography. As a structured narrative hagiography creates its

[32] Kelly MB, *Seduced by Grace: Contemporary Spirituality, Gay Experience, and Christian Faith* (Melbourne: Clouds of Magellan Press, 2007).
[33] ibid.
[34] Althaus-Reid M, *The Queer God* (New York: Routledge, 2004), 50.

own 'chrononormativity': a pattern of saintly behaviour measured by the unfolding of a set of mileposts which create a normative saintly journey through time.[35] There is an *inevitability* in the trajectory of their life that presents them as straight arrows shot through time to eternal glory. As an accounting of perfection their lives are confined to play out against a specified set of rituals, a specified set of gender markers, and a certain set of embodiments in time. There are those who, like Joan of Arc, break from these constraints but when this happens the mechanics of saint-making work hard to redeem or rewrite the broken timelines. The fact that Joan was condemned as a heretic before she was redeemed as a saint, points to the difficulties in recognising saintliness against the grain.[36]

For the queer saint who, by definition, lives outside the steadying grid of chrononormativity there can be no straight arrow through time towards saintliness. There are only detours. Detours which become pathways. Jose Esteban Muñoz pairs queer failure with queer virtuosity as an almost infinite double helix:

> Straight time … is laden with temporal obstacles and challenges that ensure a certain kind of queer failure is axiomatic for the queer subject and collectivity. Within straight time the queer can only fail; thus, an aesthetic of failure can be productively occupied by the queer artist for the purpose of delineating the bias that underlies straight times measure … queer failure is not an aesthetic failure but instead a political refusal. It is a going off script … The other side of the performance of failure is queer virtuosity … queer utopia is not just a

---

[35] Freeman E, *Time Binds* (Durham, NC: Duke University Press, 2010).
[36] In Joan's case we see several mechanisms in operation. Both her hagiography and her condemnation as a heretic make a great deal of Joan's voices and her claim that what unfolded against norms was at the request of God. This authorises her misbehaviour and reinserts her on the traditional timeline of the saint obeying the will of God no matter how cryptic his commands. The other mechanism is that her personal timeline is transposed against the larger salvation timeline of empire and God's grand plan for favoured nations. She was condemned in 1431 and even though she was exonerated by a papal court in 1456 her cult didn't emerge until the nineteenth century when in post revolution France her story became politically useful again. She was not canonised until 1920. See Taylor LJ, 'Joan of Arc, the Church, and the Papacy, 1429-1920', *The Catholic Historical Review*, 98(2), 2012, 217-240 for an analysis of her trials and retrials.

failure to achieve normative virtuosity; it is also a virtuosity which is born in the face of failure within straight time's measure.[37]

Although many of the measures of chrononormativity – notably marriage and parenting – have been queered, the inevitability of failure for the queer subject located in a straight place and time is still very real for many people. It is particularly acute for the queer Christian who is still set up to fail from an early age by the antagonism between the knowing desire of his/her body and the constraining condemnations of the church. But for the queer saint, what starts as a construction of self as a failed Christian can transform into an experience of queer virtuosity. The queer (failed) saint recognises this rupture as grace.

In describing one of his interviewees in *Christian Mysticism's Queer Flame*, Michael notes that in his twenties Joe 'struggled with deep interior darkness as his boyhood faith was deconstructed.'[38] This pattern is evident in most of the gay men Michael interviews; he talks of three awakenings, the awakening of spirituality, the awakening of sexuality and the awakening to 'the clash, within themselves between these two energies.'[39] In negotiating these three awakenings these men create what one of them, Mike, called a 'self-validating' relationship to both sexuality and spirit. After Mike had a deep sexual encounter for the first time, there was no longer any question that this could be a failed experience:

> At that point, there was such a sense of naturalness, sense of coming home to myself, that almost from that moment on I could never take seriously any of the natural law arguments you would find in Roman Catholic teaching … The experience was so self-validating, there was such clarity about this is how I am and this is who I want to be that it just never had any traction from that point on … God was in the sheer joy of it … this was connection, this is holy stuff here, and I'm on holy ground.[40]

---

[37] Muñoz JE, *Cruising Utopia: The Then and There of Queer Futurity* (New York: NYU Press, 2019), 173-78.

[38] Kelly MB, *Christian Mysticism's Queer Flame: Spirituality in the Lives of Contemporary Gay Men* (New York: Routledge, 2018), 103.

[39] ibid., 174.

[40] ibid., 123.

Joe describes an almost mystical coming out to himself and how he claimed in that moment a new sense of interior power:

> I remember there was this … voice is too literal … pressure maybe, something interior, that said, 'Say it, voice it'. I did, in the middle of that meditation, I literally … the words came out of my mouth, 'I'm gay'. That was the very first time I said that, I remember just completely breaking down – it was like a liberating feeling … thank God I've made it past that, I've finally got it out … there was a feeling of, 'Say it because you're loved, because you can say it, and you don't need to keep denying this'. I knew that what I was saying was contrary to church teaching, but was equally convinced that it was not contrary to what God wanted for me. There was that inner decision to say, 'I trust my inner experience of God, of love', rather than to trust the church.[41]

These 'self-validating' interior experiences are only one part of the queer spiritual journey and what is equally fascinating in the lives of the men that Michael interviews is the diverse pathways from these moments of insight to lives of queer virtuosity or what Michael calls 'integration'. As one of them, Chris, notes and as is evident in many of the interviews, such integration can come at a great cost: 'It is like the 'rich young man' who is asked to sell everything and follow Jesus. It is, in a sense, being willing to risk everything for your happiness …'[42]

Glen also tells a similar story of risking everything and links this with the eruption of sex. He recalls that as a young man doing the Spiritual Exercises of St Ignatius he prayed for the 'Third Degree of Humility,' the path of suffering and disgrace. He then says: 'And believe me or not, that prayer does come true, and I have to remind myself – I prayed for that. It has everything to do with the wild adventure I call my life …'[43] Michael notes that Glen attributes his 'capacity to surrender again and again, and to let go of life-choices he had poured himself into,' to the twin influences of reading the mystics and what he calls the disruption of sex. Glen explains:

---

[41] ibid.
[42] ibid., 145.
[43] ibid., 150.

> The messiness of sex disrupts everything, and the messiness of sex in
> spirituality is the key thing . . . I would call it a queer eruption . . .
> and that's good, it lets all that ego just kind of explode and it gets
> constructed in new configurations and new ways and thoughts. It is
> what we talk about when we talk about freedom.[44]

We see in the lives of these gay men, Michael's future queer saints, the
dialectic of queer failure and queer virtuosity and for most of these men the
pathway towards integration is not linear. Michael discusses the case of
David at length.[45] We can recognise in David many of the models of both
traditional and queer sanctity. In terms of a traditional hagiography there is a
sense of the sacred that glimmered in his life from an early age. There is an
attempt at a traditional priestly religious life that ends in a confrontation
with his sexuality. Out of this failure he reconfigures a life and a new sense
of the sacred. There are various points of transformation, both ecstatic
experiences and dark nights. He builds a career as a psychotherapist and at
the height of the AIDS crisis in New York David is a person for others,
engaged in both activism and pastoral care. It appears that he is a model of
integration who learns from queer failure and models a type of queer
virtuosity 'born in the face of failure within straight time's measure.'[46] But in
his late fifties both his professional and his spiritual life is destabilised, and
he must begin again. When he breaks through this challenge into a new
ecstatic wholeness, an unexpected impasse arises. What initially causes this
new dark night is a sudden realisation, a dreadful epiphany. As a client is
describing his desire to 'touch another man's genitals' David experiences a
strange visceral reaction that disturbs his sense of spiritual equanimity, and
he realises that his spiritual 'purification project' still somehow sits uneasily
with his publicly integrated sexuality. He realises at this point that his
'purification project is bankrupt'. He continues:

> How it gets replaced is beyond me, but I know it's bankrupt and it's
> been the great project of my life. What must replace it is an infusion
> of – grace. I don't know what grace is, I know I'm not the author of
> grace, like I know I'm not the author of this beyond beautiful

---

[44] ibid.
[45] ibid., 157-61.
[46] Muñoz JE, *Cruising Utopia: The Then and There of Queer Futurity* (New York: NYU Press, 2019), 178.

cosmos, I'm not the author of it, I'm a creature in it and of it, I'm a creature of its creator … I do know that that to which I'm present is not in the shape or form of that which my mind knows. And that's a peaceful thing for me, and to the degree that I can place myself there, I don't want anything else. I can't place myself there all the time … [47]

This strange place of not-knowing, of failure, of being out-of-time, or being in that time-which-is-left, this is the place of queer saintliness, a saintliness that no longer relies on the easy tropes of hagiography. This is David's place beyond purification; this is the place of Pauli Murray's dark night of gender; this is Mychal Judge's place of service in brokenness; this is the aching-time that came to Matt Shepard with such shocking suddenness that night in Wyoming.

Conclusion

In talking of saints, even queer ones or postmodern ones, there is always the danger of talking too glibly of redemptive suffering. These radical new beings are born of suffering, but their response is not just passive acquiescence, 'offering it up' in the traditional model, it is the call as Muñoz suggests to resistance: 'to go off script'. As Marcella Althaus-Reid put it we must claim rebelliousness as core to saintliness. [48]

Constance Fitzgerald, one of the mystical theologians that Michael draws on in his study, points out that the mystical dark night is not just an individual experience of abnegation. She refers to 'the dark night of the world' [49] facing ecological disaster, and the dark 'night of broken symbols' [50] which create an impasse for disenfranchised groups like women or queers in the church. Saintly innovators experience the depth of this ecological and social void not just as it affects them but as it affects all of us, and they register this darkness as a call to action. As Fitzgerald ponders:

> What if, by chance, our time in evolution is a dark-night time – a time of crisis and transition that must be understood if it is to be part

---

[47] Kelly MB, *Christian Mysticism's Queer Flame: Spirituality in the Lives of Contemporary Gay Men* (New York: Routledge, 2018), 160-1.
[48] Althaus-Reid M, *The Queer God* (New York: Routledge, 2004).
[49] Fitzgerald C, 'Impasse and Dark Night' in Edwards T (ed.), *Living with Apocalypse* (San Francisco: Harper & Row, 1984), 94.
[50] ibid., 110.

of learning a new vision and harmony for the human species and the planet?[51]

Learning and embodying that new vision, what Michael, following Simone Weil, calls saintly genius, is not just based on the singularity of saintly lives, it is based on the recognition and the practice that occurs in their wake. What Wyschogrod has called their 'radical altruism' is perhaps ultimately defined by the fact that not even death puts an end to this gifting of self for others.

This essay has been written, as I stated at its beginning, in conversation with Michael Kelly's life and theologising. The purpose of this essay is not to canonise him, but it is to call out and celebrate his life, which was a life, lived and broken open for others and like a saint's life, the gift of Michael's life remains a fierce power in our world today.

Can a queer person become a saint? Yes, they can, and Michael's work shows us, in a detailed and intimate way, something of the inner beauty of fully sexualised queer holiness.

---

[51] ibid., 94.

For Lo, The Winter has Passed

Will Day

The original version of this piece was shared at Michael's funeral.

As our queer Godfather, North American poet and mystic Walt Whitman, reminded us, '*we contain multitudes*', and Michael, like most of us, has many aspects. I'd like to say a little about a couple of those aspects which I greatly appreciate.

We first met at a cafe by the sea in Elwood about twenty-five years ago, one of many meetings in cafes overlooking Michael's beloved Port Phillip Bay. As we parted that day he said, 'Let's stay in touch, it's always good to meet another contemplative.'

I wasn't sure that I identified with that label, but Michael knew he had a contemplative heart. Although he had his insecurities and doubts Michael had a confidence, a pride and dignity about who he was, about his calling, and his mission. And he extended this dignity, pride and confidence to include his queer community; he insisted we be respected, and he was indignant at any affront to us. He was, and is, in so many ways our champion. And I believe that this conviction, this self-belief and belief in his community, was anchored in his contemplative heart.

Part of Michael's consciousness, it seemed to me, was abiding in, being nourished and energised by very deep pools: all those hours spent wandering the lonely coastal beaches, times alone in prayer, reflection and at times great struggle. Countless hours sitting by himself in a cafe, sipping coffee and quietly gazing out at the waters of the Bay …

In the little contemplative classic 'The Cloud of Unknowing' the author entreats us; '*Leave my contemplatives alone. Leave them to their sitting, resting and enjoying, you don't know what is happening to them*'.

*

One of the precious things about Michael was that he both abided in those depths and worked deeply in our ordinary world.

I'd like to mention some small but telling examples of Michael's deep work; examples of the great, mysterious Love that lies at the heart of our lives, that Michael was inspired by, and that dances up through us and out into the world.

I found it very moving to hear my dear friend Patricia describe Michael's visit to her elderly mother's hospital bed. Patricia's mother Marie had lived a very long and good life, but she was agitated and anxious as she approached death. Her family, gathered around her in the hospital, were also anxious and on edge. Most of the family had never met Michael.

Patricia describes how Michael entered the room, sat beside her dying mother, took her hand and together they began praying the rosary. Patricia was profoundly moved by the way the room quieted, everyone gradually settled, and Marie relaxed into a deep peace. When it was time for Michael to leave, Marie didn't want to let go of his hand.

After Michael had left, Patricia's brother who she describes as a 'bah humbug atheist' turned to her, amazed, saying; 'Who was that guy?!!'

I'm reminded of the first line of the prayer of Michael's beloved Francis of Assisi; *'Make me an instrument of your peace.'*

About 10 years ago I was at a Radical Faeries gathering at the Abbotsford Convent. I got talking with one of the faery men sitting nearby and our conversation led me to ask him if he had read *Seduced by Grace* by Michael Kelly. There was a pause after which he replied, 'Yesterday morning I was sitting in a cafe reading that book, and weeping.'

I wonder how many people, and how many gay men, have been deeply moved or brought to tears by Michael's writing, his workshops, his liturgies or conversations? Those tears, as far as I can see, are holy tears; tears of cleansing, of healing, of bringing in the new, of reclaiming life.

Michael's work reverberates and ripples out and I believe it will continue to do so.

In 2009 the World Parliament of Religions met in Melbourne. Over 6000 people attended, and hundreds of talks and events were offered, centred around the Exhibition Centre in Southbank.

Michael saw an early draft of the program and at that time there were no LGBTIQ events offered. Michael immediately went to work to address what to him was a completely disrespectful omission.

On a cloudy Saturday morning Michael, myself and two others sat in a reasonably sized room preparing the session. I thought perhaps a handful of people would show up; it was a Saturday; the venue was very busy with about 30 other sessions scheduled at the same time as ours. But our session was packed and very lively, with people standing at the back. We heard story after story describing grief and hurt, yet the room was filled with joy and a kind of bubbling delight because we had gathered together, scores of queer folk from all over the world, acknowledging and sharing our religious and spiritual experiences.

Conversations were had, connections were made, the channels of healing and change were enlivened and a whole new set of reverberations were set in motion. Thanks to Michael Kelly.

How often over the past 30 years has a version of this pattern been repeated: Michael's seed, once planted, sprouts and flourishes thereby enabling other seeds to be planted, to sprout and to grow.

*

Michael lived with various health issues. The one that made its way into our conversations most often was Chronic Fatigue Syndrome, a condition we shared. When talking about Michael, about the shape of his life and his many achievements, it would be neglectful to omit the heavy and pervasive burden his health circumstances placed on his life, his well-being, his choices and relationships. It seems to me impressive that he achieved all he did, weighed down as he was. His suffering ought to be noted and remembered; it was with him every day for many, many years.

When Michael was applying to do his PhD at Monash University, we met for coffee one afternoon at the Rivoli in Camberwell. As we chatted Michael began to express his concerns about his upcoming academic endeavour; 'I don't know if I have the mental acuity.' Missing his point, I hastened to reassure him; 'Michael! You're an intelligent man!'. He became quiet and solemn; 'I'm not talking about intelligence.'

Michael knew that complex thought – and retaining, reflecting on and refining one's complex thought – requires a great deal of mental agility and energy, both of which were sorely hampered by the uncommon fatigue which dogged him, impeding his cognitive functioning, his insights, his intellectual gifts. This is a phenomenon which affects many who live with chronic health issues: a keen awareness of their capacities and potentials and an equally keen sense of their inability to live them.

Despite this, Michael completed his doctorate. As he was writing up his research, and putting together the thesis, he lamented that the final product could not be what he would have liked it to be, could not go where he should have liked it to go. It was a definite compromise to his considerable limitations. Nevertheless, to his credit, he still produced an important, exciting, pioneering document which went on to become his last book; 'Christian Mysticism's Queer Flame'. (Michael had called it simply 'Queer

Flame of Love', a title his publishers felt may mislead potential readers who were likely to mistake it for some kind of queer, racy Mills and Boon romance!)

I recall conversations we would have when Michael was preparing to go overseas. As he prepared to take up a residency at a theological college in the US, we discussed how he might shape his day. Michael wondered if he would have the strength and clarity of mind to fulfil his obligation to engage appropriately in the intellectual life of the place; 'Well perhaps if I rest until late afternoon, I might have the energy to engage for a couple of hours in the evening.'

And there were conversations in the weeks leading up to his long-haul flights from Melbourne to the US when Michael was particularly fatigued and wondering how on earth he might pack, drag himself to the plane and then do the necessary travelling and settling at the other end. It seems he usually managed but there was often a price to pay; the need to plan for some days of rest and no commitments when he reached his destination; and when he finally returned home to Australia, the need for a week in his burrow.

Michael felt a deep affinity with the dark night of the contemplative life, the territory where God and God's consolations seem to be far away, and where doubt may begin to question whether they ever existed at all. Some contemplatives live a life enriched by profound inner experiences of peace, joy and the felt touch of divine love. In the Christian tradition such experiences are referred to as consolations, and for someone whose life involves considerable suffering such consolations can provide great comfort, reassurance and replenishment, making it more possible to go on and encounter the next difficult day.

Michael however made it very clear at times that such consolations were not generally part of his contemplative path; on various occasions he referred to barrenness, to God's absence. Which to me makes his conviction and his faith all the more impressive and, in a way, curious. I find myself wondering just what the elements were, biographical and otherwise, constellating around Michael's contemplative nature to shape his particular spiritual conviction, motivation and priestly personhood.

*

Michael died last Saturday morning. I heard the news on the Sunday afternoon but when I sat to meditate on the Saturday evening, and began to include Michael in my prayers, as so many of us have been doing over the months, I was surprised by the sense of an open, clear, clean space and the definite impression that this man did not need prayers, that he was completely OK. The same thing happened on the Sunday morning. When I heard on Sunday afternoon that Michael had died it all made sense.

So, in the spirit of that experience, and in acknowledgment of Michael's request, his insistence, that we ought to embrace and celebrate beautiful, gritty eros in both its earthiness and its Divinity, I would like to close with these lines of joyous arrival, of love and Springtime, from the Song of Solomon:

> My beloved spoke, and said unto me,
> rise up my love, my fair one, and come away.
> For, lo, the winter is past, the rain is over and gone;
> the flowers appear on the earth;
> and the time of the singing of birds is come. Alleluia.
> And the voice of the turtle is heard in our land;
> the fig tree putteth forth her green figs,
> and the vines with the tender grape give a good smell.
> Arise my love, my fair one, and come away.
> My beloved is mine, and I am his. Alleluia

I already miss Michael, and yet he is still here.

Acknowledgements

Noelene Kelly

On behalf of Michael's family, especially my sister, Maureen Kelly Kocz, and my brother, Brian Kelly, I offer thanks and acknowledgement to all who made this collection of essays a reality.

Into Your Hands began as a conversation at Michael's wake. We were gathered on the deck of a cafe overlooking the waters of Port Phillip Bay and just a few sand dunes away from Portsea Ocean Beach – where Michael would regularly pause at the close of the day and offer his sunset prayer. Talk on the deck that day was filled with sadness, but also with a determination to advance the legacy of Michael's thought and work. At the centre of this conversation was Dr Maria Pallotta-Chiarolli.

Maria had known Michael since the mid-1990s when he was settling back into Melbourne after his years of study and campus ministry in San Francisco. Maria's outstanding body of work – writing, research, teaching and advocacy – on issues of cultural diversity and inclusion, and her championing of the rights of LGBTIQ+ young people, had many natural connection points with Michael's radical and prophetic challenge to the Catholic Church on issues concerning the integration of sexuality and spirituality.

It was Maria who proposed the idea of this essay collection. Her vision and her ongoing enthusiasm for this project have been critical to its unfolding. Her interview with Nan McGregor on which the essay *Something I Had to Do* is based speaks to the refinement and delicacy of her skills and her deep solidarity with those engaged in the work of justice and inclusion.

Gordon Thompson has been a champion of Michael's thought and writing since first publishing *Seduced by Grace* in 2007, a collection of Michael's essays, articles and letters. As the founding director of Clouds of Magellan Press, he has since published a study guide to Michael's video lecture series *The Erotic Contemplative* (2020). In 2021 he published an updated edition of *Seduced by Grace*, and a book version of *The Erotic Contemplative* to mark the first anniversary of Michael's death. Gordon has also been a valued touchstone – wise and generous – for both Andrew Brown as editor, and for me as family representative and overseer of Michael's literary estate. Without Gordon's input and counsel, this project would not have been possible. I offer deep gratitude to him and to his partner Petrina Barson for many levels of assistance and for providing a platform over many years for alternative and marginalised voices. My thanks also to Helen Bell who has edited many of Michael's published works, and who cast her experienced eye over the final draft of this collection.

Andrew Brown, who was part of the conversation on the deck at Michael's wake, has brought editorial expertise and energy to this project. His communication skills, along with his intuitive feel for the material, have produced an essay collection that is fluent and cohesive. He has remained true to Michael's often stated view that writing should be clear and accessible regardless of the sophistication or complexity of the content. I thank him for committing in such a heartfelt way to this essay collection.

My thanks to Ro Allen for their thoughtful and generous introduction to this collection and for their crucial work in advocacy and inclusion in their role as Victorian Equal Opportunity and Human Rights Commissioner.

I thank Eureka O'Hanlon for generously allowing his artwork, *Hand of Job,* to grace the cover of this collection. This image was much loved by Michael, speaking as it does to the naked, embodied yearning of the human heart.

Jim Nickoloff suggested that the title of this collection include the words 'mystic' and 'prophet', as Michael 'combined these two vocations in an extraordinary way'. I thank Jim for his insight and his loving insistence on this matter.

My deepest gratitude goes to all contributors. As soon as the call went out for contributions to a proposed essay collection in honour of Michael, responses were immediate. Many writers made contributions in the midst of substantial professional or personal pressures, and I thank them for the quality and care of their submissions. I am especially indebted to those who created new works for this collection. To those who brought previously published or presented works into dialogue with Michael's thought, my thanks for the illuminative spark and richness revealed by these conversations.

It speaks to Michael's breadth of influence that these essays span such a time frame and such diverse perspectives. It is through the words of each writer, through their memories and engaged reflections, that we glimpse the wide-ranging impact of Michael and his work. Most importantly, we are offered unique insights into what his life's work might mean and how it might continue to effect change in our individual lives and in the communal networks of which we are part.

Our ultimate debt, of course, is to Michael himself. Beyond his brilliance and his creative giftedness, he was, like all of us, flawed and incomplete, alive to his own wounds and shortcomings. And yet, in the midst of it all, he lived his 'Fiat' – his 'yes' – in every challenge that emerged in his life, and in the final 'dance' that led to his death. Always before him was the vivifying presence of Francesco, and of Jesus his Beloved, in whose passionate embrace he sought to live the fullness of his humanity and bear witness to Divine Love – that 'mystery ever ancient, ever new, that is manifesting in every moment, in every being, in every beat of every human heart'.[1]

As one of Michael's dear NYC friends, Kevin Tortorelli OFM, commented just after his death, 'Michael was to me always a friar minor in his concern for the disenfranchised, the abandoned, the sick, the misunderstood, the persecuted. He was their champion. This extended to the Earth in deep appreciation of our home. He foresaw many of the issues that now more broadly concern us. He rejoiced to see people healed, free and joyful. Within these perspectives he loved the Church and saw how deep the need for a true and vital reform is, a roaring big conversion to greater and wider hearts.'

May these essays fuel that 'roaring big conversion' within our churches and beyond. May we all be inspired towards 'greater and wider hearts' by the words and ideas collected here.

It goes without saying that Michael would never have imagined that his life, much less his death, would inspire an essay collection such as this. He would be deeply humbled.

My thanks to all.

Mazel Tov, my brother.

Noelene Kelly

---

[1] Kelly MB, *Seduced by Grace: Contemporary Spirituality, Gay Experience, and Christian Faith* (Melbourne: Clouds of Magellan Press, 2021), xviii.

Contributors

Petrina Barson

Petrina Barson is the director of the Centre for a Compassionate Society. She is also a mother, doctor, trauma therapist, poet, activist, and senior teacher of the Compassion Institute's 'Compassion Cultivation Training'.
https://centreforacompassionatesociety.net

Andrew Brown

Andrew Brown is from Detroit, Michigan, USA. He studied religion and sexuality at the University of Michigan, in part to deepen his understanding of his own experiences as a gay Catholic. He received a master of social work from Washington University in St. Louis. In 2015, Andrew moved to Melbourne for a research position in community-led health and wellbeing at Deakin University. Andrew is grateful to Michael Kelly for welcoming him into Melbourne's queer and spiritual community.

Leslie Cartwright

Leslie Cartwright is a voice teacher specialising in actor-training. He has coached many of Australia's leading performers on stage and screen.

Beth R. Crisp

Beth Crisp is Professor of Social Work and Deputy Head of the School of Health and Social Development at Deakin University. Working at the interface between religion and social welfare practice, her work explores how faith-based responses can address social exclusion for people who find themselves on the margins of the Church or wider society.

Greg Curran

Dr. Greg Curran is a teacher who is passionate about social justice in education. He has taught in the primary, TAFE and university sectors. His interests are literacy and numeracy, gender and sexual diversity, cultural diversity, Indigenous Australian history, climate change, and building more inclusive learning spaces in education. Greg hosts and produces the education-focused podcast, Pushing The Edge with Greg Curran, and writes on teaching and social justice issues at pushingtheedge.org.

Will Day

Will Day lives by the Yarra River in the suburbs of Melbourne. Will considers Michael his 'queer, contemplative ally and friend'. Will is a Camaldolese Oblate, creative arts therapist and writer who lives with chronic fatigue syndrome.

Paul Gates

Paul is the eldest of eight children. He and Michael first met in 1972 when they both joined the Franciscans. In 1977, Paul left the Order, as Michael had done some years earlier. He spent several years doing welfare work in a large men's hostel and then trained as a secondary teacher. He taught Religious Education, Science and History, in Sydney Catholic schools for 14 years and for another 22 years in Cairns, before retiring in 2017. He married in 1983 and he and his wife have 3 children (now adults) and still live in Cairns.

Peter Gates

Peter came to know and establish a friendship with Michael during Michael's time with the Franciscans and afterwards, when Michael lived in Sydney in the 1970s.

Mark Gates

Mark also became a friend of Michael's during Michael's time in the Franciscans and afterwards. Mark studied to be a lawyer and still practises in Sydney today.

Mark Jordan

Mark D. Jordan is Niebuhr Research Professor at Harvard Divinity School. He writes about the prospects for Christian sexual ethics, the arts of religious teaching, and the languages of queer spirituality.

Noelene J. Kelly

Noelene is a Melbourne teacher and writer. She holds a PhD in ecological literature and has a deep connection to the Mornington Peninsula and Victoria's high country. The love she shares with her brother, Michael, has over the years been sustaining, maddening, sacrament, grace!

Bernard J. Lynch

Bernard J. Lynch has an interdisciplinary doctorate in counselling psychology and theology from Fordham University and New York Theological Seminary. For fifteen years he was Theological Consultant to the Board of Directors of Dignity

New York – an organisation for LGBTQI+ Catholics and their friends. He founded the AIDS/HIV Ministry of Dignity New York in 1982, which continues its work to the present day. It was through Bernard's work in New York that he first met Michael. Later on, Michael visited and stayed with Bernard and his husband Billy in London which is where they presently reside. Web address: www.frbernardlynch.com

Anthony McAleer

Anthony McAleer OAM attended Aquinas College, Ringwood, for his secondary education where Michael Kelly was his influential English teacher. He later went on to complete a BA in History at Monash University and a career with Museums Victoria and has written or edited twenty-four books, mainly to do with the history of the Yarra Valley. He was awarded Shire of Yarra Ranges Citizen of the Year in 1997, a centenary of Federation medal for community service in 2001 and a Medal of the Order of Australia in 2018 for community service and contributions to military history.

Nanette McGregor

Nan McGregor is an icon of the LGBTIQ+ community in Melbourne. Considered by many to be the 'patron saint' of young gay men and lesbians, she was the President of the Victorian chapter of PFLAG (Parents and Friends of Lesbian and Gay children) for almost 10 years. Politicised by the bullying and discrimination experienced by her son Kieran because of his sexual identity, she became an influential voice in the movement for equality and inclusion. This demand also extended to her church community. It was in this context that she met Michael who, at the time of their meeting, was in the process of co-founding the Rainbow Sash Movement. Nan's justice work was expansive, and continued to her death in April 2022. A remarkable woman and a shining soul, her legacy will continue to enrich us all. We are honoured to have Nan's words and reflections as part of this collection.

Constant J. Mews

Professor Constant J. Mews FAHA has been Director of the Centre for Religious Studies at Monash University since 1995. He is a medievalist by training, with a special interest in intellectual life and religious thought in medieval Europe, with particular reference to Abelard and Heloise, Hildegard of Bingen, Bernard of Clairvaux, and their contemporaries. He is also strongly interested in issues of interreligious dialogue.

Jay Michaelson

Rabbi Dr. Jay Michaelson is a visiting fellow at the Center for LGBTQ Studies in Religion (CLGS), Pacific School of Religion, Berkeley, California, as well as an author (*God vs. Gay? The Religious Case for Equality*), journalist (columnist, *New York Magazine*) and meditation teacher (senior editor, Ten Percent Happier). He holds a PhD in Jewish Thought from Hebrew University, a JD from Yale, and nondenominational rabbinic ordination. Previously, Jay worked as a professional LGBTQ activist for ten years, founding two religious LGBTQ non-profits and speaking at over 100 religious institutions. After meeting Michael at the 2003 Gay Spirit Culture summit, Jay worked closely with him at Easton Mountain Retreat Center and on numerous initiatives to bridge the perceived gaps between traditional religions and liberated sexuality.

Darren Nash

Darren Nash is an alumnus of the Aquinas College Class of 84 and had the honour of being taught English by Michael Kelly in Year Ten, being directed by him in the school production, *Jesus Christ Superstar*, in Year Eleven and the great privilege of counting him as a friend thereafter.

James B. Nickoloff

James B. Nickoloff is Associate Professor Emeritus of Religious Studies at the College of the Holy Cross in Worcester, Massachusetts, where he taught Catholic systematic theology from 1989 to 2009. He is currently Director of Ministerial Formation at Barry University in Miami, Florida where he has been teaching theology since 2009. He has lived and worked for extended periods outside his native United States, including three years in Andong, Korea as a Peace Corps Volunteer; two years in Kingston, Jamaica as a Jesuit; and two years in Lima, Peru, where he wrote his doctoral dissertation. In recent years he has taught at Boston College, Weston Jesuit School of Theology, Santa Clara University in the U.S., and at the Jesuit Theological College in Melbourne, Australia. He has worked extensively with Catholic high school principals, teachers, students, and boards of trustees in Victoria and other Australian states. He is the editor of *Gustavo Gutiérrez: Essential Writings* (1996), the editor of *In, Out, and About on the Hill: LGBTQIA+ Alums Reflect on Life at Holy Cross* (1978-2018) (2019), and the co-editor with Orlando Espín of *An Introductory Dictionary of Theology and Religious Studies* (winner of the 2007 Catholic Press Association Book Award). He has also published analytical essays on ecclesiology, the theological vision of Gutiérrez, and the various theologies of liberation.

Marcus O'Donnell

Professor Marcus O'Donnell is a Melbourne writer, artist and academic. He got to know Michael when, as editor of *OutRage* and *Sydney Star Observer*, he commissioned Michael to write a number of essays. He and Michael discovered a shared history as gay Catholics who had been drawn deeply to the monastic tradition. Michael weaved in and out of Marcus' life for twenty years as he visited Sydney and then again when Marcus, more recently, moved back to Melbourne. There were long gaps where they had no contact, but it was always easy to begin that single long conversation again when they reconnected. Marcus' essays continue that conversation. He is currently Professor of Higher Education at Navitas, Australia.

Eureka O'Hanlon

Eureka O'Hanlon initially trained as a social worker and manager. Eureka uses his art-making to come out as a gay man, a continuing process of countering the assumptions of everyday life. As a queer artist, his mission is to find those things hidden in plain sight, such as his exploration of the homoeroticism in Catholic art. He likes to create new possibilities through his art, imagining a future freer and more inclusive than the present. Eureka captures the male form in a variety of media including photomontage, life drawing, and remote drawing via zoom. He has completed artists' residencies in Berlin in 2014, Venice in 2016, USA in 2017, Spain in 2018 and Greece in 2019. Eureka loves to share his creativity with others; he has taught life drawing at festivals and art schools for over a decade. In 2020, he produce his first art book, *Ecce Homo Corona,* dedicated to Michael Bernard Kelly.

Benjamin Oh

Benjamin Oh is a member of the Committee for the Australian LGBTIQ Multicultural Council (AGMC) and the Gay and Lesbian Rights Lobby of New South Wales (GLRL). Benjamin was the Founding Secretary of the Global Network of Rainbow Catholics (GNRC). Amongst the organisations he founded are: the Rainbow Catholics InterAgency for Ministry (RCiA) bringing together affirming LGBTIQ Catholic ministries around Australia to advance justice with LGBTIQ folks; Equal Voices – the national ecumenical LGBTIQ Christian organisation; and the Asian Australian Alliance. Ben is a proud father of two wonderful children and has been with his spouse Nam for 16 years. Ben first met Michael at an Acceptance Melbourne home Mass two decades ago.

Maria Pallotta-Chiarolli

Dr Maria Pallotta-Chiarolli is an academic, author, ally and activist. An Honorary Fellow in the School of Communication and Creative Arts, Deakin University, she also has her own consultancy, GSE Tapestry Consulting. Maria is also a founding member of the Australian LGBTIQ+ Multicultural Council since 2004, and has collaborated in many research projects, events and training for AGMC over the years, including chief editing work on the AGMC anthology, *Living and Loving in Diversity: An Anthology of Australian Multicultural Queer Adventures* (2018). Maria won the Victorian Globe Straight Ally Award in 2018 and has been honoured with a Fellowship in her name from the Centre for Writers, WA. She was recently appointed a Member of the Order of Australia (AM) in the 2022 Australia Day Honours for her 'significant service to the LGBTIQ community, and to education'.

Kate Rigby

Professor Dr. Kate Rigby (Fellow of the Australian Academy of the Humanities) is Alexander von Humboldt Professor of Environmental Humanities at the University of Cologne, where she directs the research hub for Multidisciplinary Environmental Studies in the Humanities (MESH). Her research lies at the intersection of environmental literary, philosophical, historical and religious studies, with a specialist interest in European Romanticism, ecopoetics, and eco-catastrophe. A founding co-editor of the journal *Philosophy Activism Nature*, she is co-editor of the University Press of Virginia series, Under the Sign of Nature, and her books include *Topographies of the Sacred: The Poetics of Place in European Romanticism* (2004), *Dancing with Disaster: Environmental Histories, Narratives, and Ethics for Perilous Times* (2015) and *Reclaiming Romanticism: Towards an Ecopoetics of Decolonization* (2020). A key researcher with the Humanities for the Environment Mellon Australia-Pacific Observatory, she was the inaugural President of the Association for the Study of Literature, Environment and Culture (Australia-New Zealand), and the founding Director of the Australia-Pacific Forum on Religion and Ecology. She had the honour of supervising Michael Kelly's PhD thesis, *Queer Flame of Love: Re-imagining the Christian Mystical Tradition in Light of the Experience of Contemporary Gay Men* (Centre for Religious Studies, Monash University 2014).

John Xavier Rolley

John was first ordained in 2001 as a priest with the Ecumenical Catholic Church of Australia, an open and inclusive independent catholic jurisdiction. In addition to working with people on the margins of society, John served alongside Bishop Michael Kelly from 2011 in several contexts including Inclusive Catholics and the Emmaus Community. John's primary focus has been the development of inclusive liturgy for contemporary Eucharistic communities. John is also a nurse with 19 years of academic nursing practice. He completed his PhD in 2009. John is currently in formation for the Anglican priesthood.

Abanob Saad

Abanob Saad is a Coptic (Egyptian) Orthodox gay man who breathes advocacy, champions justice, and dreams of a future where Eastern LGBTI+ people can hold their faith and sexuality comfortably without hate, prejudice, or exclusion. As a survivor of insidious conversion therapy, he founded Queer Middle Eastern and African Christians in Australia (QMEACA). Abanob was ministerially appointed to sit on the Victorian Government LGBTIQ Taskforce, and is now a teacher in a Melbourne secondary school.

Christian Scharen

Christian Scharen was ordained a pastor in the Evangelical Lutheran Church in America (ELCA) in 2001. He holds a Ph.D. in Religion from Emory University and has written or edited more than a dozen books and many articles, book chapters, and research reports on religious organizations, religion and culture, LGBTQ inclusion, social justice, and theological education. His book on gay marriage, *Married in the Sight of God* (2000) helped spark the movement towards the ELCA's current open and affirming stance towards LGBTQ persons. His most recent book, *Someone Has to Care: The Roots and Hip-Hop's Prophetic Calling*, was released in November 2021. His current research project is a decolonial theological memoir about his family, the Ingalls family of *The Little House on the Prairie* series.

Works by Michael Bernard Kelly

Seduced by Grace: Contemporary spirituality, Gay experience, and Christian faith by Michael Bernard Kelly

Clouds of Magellan Press (2021). Originally published in 2007, *Seduced by Grace* is now available internationally as a paperback in an updated edition. ISBN: 978-0-6451935-2-7. First edition available as ebook.

The Erotic Contemplative: Reflections on the Spiritual Journey of the Gay/Lesbian Christian by Michael Bernard Kelly

Clouds of Magellan Press (2021). In 1994, Michael Bernard Kelly recorded six video lectures for the Erospirit Research Institute. The lectures, originally released in 1995, were digitised and re-released in 2020. Now this transcription of all the lectures is published for the first time, and includes a study guide to the series prepared by Michael Kelly.
ISBN: 978-0-6451935-7-2 – paperback
ISBN: 978-0-6451935-8-9 – ebook

Christian Mysticism's Queer Flame: Spirituality in the Lives of Contemporary Gay Men by Michael Bernard Kelly
Routledge (2019) | ISBN 978-0-3675874-4-4

www.ingramcontent.com/pod-product-compliance
Lightning Source LLC
Chambersburg PA
CBHW070034100426
42740CB00013B/2692